LOST WORLDS AND MYSTERIOUS CIVILIZATIONS

Nubia

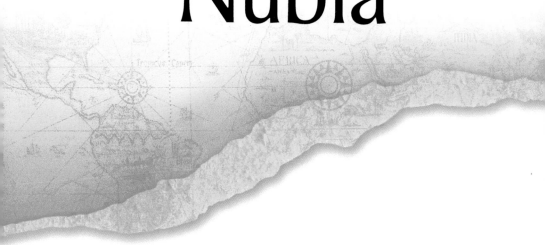

LOST WORLDS AND MYSTERIOUS CIVILIZATIONS

Atlantis

Easter Island

El Dorado

The Maya

Nubia

Pompeii

Roanoke

Troy

LOST WORLDS AND MYSTERIOUS CIVILIZATIONS

Nubia

Adam Woog

CHELSEA HOUSE
An Infobase Learning Company

Nubia

Copyright ©2012 by Infobase Learning

Chelsea House
An imprint of Infobase Learning
132 West 31st Street
New York NY 10001

Library of Congress Cataloging-in-Publication Data
Woog, Adam, 1953–
  Nubia / by Adam Woog.
      p. cm. — (Lost worlds and mysterious civilizations)
  Includes bibliographical references and index.
  ISBN-13: 978-1-60413-973-0 (hardcover)
  ISBN-10: 1-60413-973-0 (hardcover)
  1. Nubia—History—Juvenile literature. 2. Nubians—Social life and customs—Juvenile literature. I. Title. II. Series: Lost worlds and mysterious civilizations.
  DT159.6.N83W66 2011
  939'.78—dc22   2011011635

Chelsea House books are available at special discounts when purchased in bulk quantities for businesses, associations, institutions, or sales promotions. Please call our Special Sales Department in New York at (212) 967-8800 or (800) 322-8755.

You can find Chelsea House on the World Wide Web at http://www.infobaselearning.com

Text design by Erika K. Arroyo
Cover design by Alicia Post
Composition by EJB Publishing Services
Cover printed by Yurchak Printing, Landisville, Pa.
Book printed and bound by Yurchak Printing, Landisville, Pa.

Printed in the United States of America

This book is printed on acid-free paper.

All links and Web addresses were checked and verified to be correct at the time of publication. Because of the dynamic nature of the Web, some addresses and links may have changed since publication and may no longer be valid.

Contents

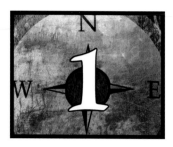

Introducing Nubia

Nubia, south of Egypt in the hot, dry lands of North Africa, was one of the most mysterious, intriguing, and important ancient civilizations in the world. It had a rich and distinctive culture far back into prehistory, at least as early as 3500 B.C., and possibly much earlier. Furthermore, Nubia was a unified, independent kingdom by about 750 B.C., making it the world's oldest known black nation.

Within Nubia's long history, several separate kingdoms rose and fell. In some cases, these kingdoms were closely connected to specific religions; for a long time, Nubia was deeply influenced by a relatively new religion called Christianity. Another era succeeded that one; this next era was also dominated by a then-new religion, Islam—a faith that proved to have staying power. Islam was so powerful a force that the vast majority of people today are Muslim in this region of modern Sudan and southern Egypt.

STAYING STRONG

Although ancient Nubia regularly came under attack from outsiders, and sometimes was dominated by them, it remained defiant and resilient for most of its existence. Its military forces were renowned for their fierceness and skill. Nubian archers were so accurate, it was said that they could shoot out the eyes of their enemies. Nubian warriors in general were so terrifying that, according to legend, even a conqueror as formidable as Alexander the Great declined to oppose them.

Through all of its colorful history, the Nubian civilization was intimately tied with that of another, more familiar culture: ancient Egypt, the land of the pharaohs and Nubia's mighty neighbor to the north. The long and complex history these two shared was a tug-of-war between war and peace. Sometimes Egypt occupied Nubia; sometimes Nubia controlled Egypt's fortunes. The connections between the realms were not always violent. Sometimes, Egyptian culture and tradition filtered down to influence Nubia; at other times, Nubian customs and practices held sway over Egypt.

And yet the civilization of Nubia has remained far less famous than that of Egypt. Its historical importance has been brought into sharp focus only in recent years. Before that, archaeologists did not realize the importance of Nubia's role in the overall history of northern Africa.

There were several reasons for this. Perhaps the most important was that little in the way of Nubian artifacts and written accounts have been uncovered. In any case, the glittering civilization of Egypt, with its pyramids and mummies and carefully preserved artifacts, has attracted a great deal of study. Archaeologist Jean Leclant, writing in *Sudan: Ancient Kingdoms of the Nile*, a book edited by Dietrich Wildung, comments, "Such was the magnificence of pharaonic Egypt . . . that for the longest time modern historians studied Egypt by itself. They did not pay attention to the fact that the Nile is a great African river [along whose route people representing different cultures could travel] and that in numerous details Egyptian civilization still bore many marks of its African origins."

THE NILE

This river, the Nile, was ancient Nubia's lifeline. Similar to Egypt, Nubia's civilization developed along the banks of the Nile as the waterway made its long way to the sea. Nearly all of the region's population clustered within 10 miles (16 kilometers) of the river's banks; beyond that were regions so dry that few humans could survive there. (The same, to a degree, is true today.)

Without the Nile, in short, no civilization could have flourished in the region. Flowing north from central Africa to the Mediterranean Sea, the Nile provided the Nubians with much of what they needed to survive. It was, of course, a vital source of water for themselves, the crops

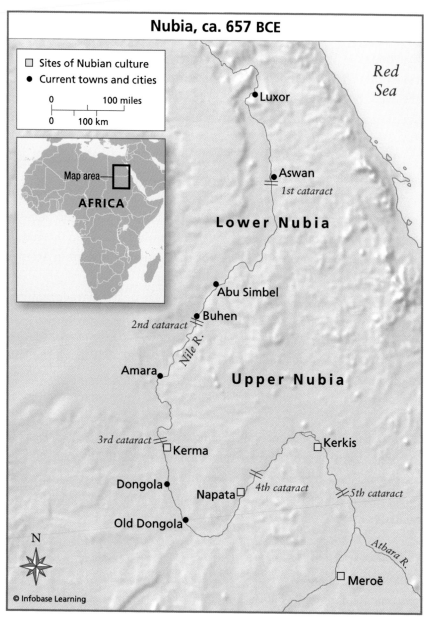

Nubia, ca. 657 BCE

☐ Sites of Nubian culture
● Current towns and cities

0   100 miles

0   100 km

Map area

AFRICA

Red Sea

● Luxor

● Aswan
1st cataract

Lower Nubia

Abu Simbel

● Buhen

2nd cataract

Nile R.

Amara ●

Upper Nubia

3rd cataract

☐ Kerma

☐ Kerkis

Dongola ●

Napata ☐   *4th cataract*

5th cataract

Old Dongola ●

N

Atbara R.

☐ Meroë

© Infobase Learning

Early people established civilizations near major bodies of water, and the Nile River was an important resource for the kingdom of Nubia. Because the Nile flowed into the Mediterranean Sea, Lower Nubia was downstream and in the north, while Upper Nubia was located in the south.

they grew, and the cattle, sheep, and other livestock they raised. But the river was far more than that. Every summer, the long Nile River Valley flooded as the river flowed down from its East African headwaters. When these floods receded, they left behind nutrients and minerals that enriched the soil and made the valley ideal for farming. A year of strong floods promised prosperity; a year with low flooding meant catastrophic drought and famine.

The Nile was also a crucial element in the economy of ancient Nubia because it was a natural travel route between Egypt and the southern regions of Africa. Pharaonic Egypt was eager to acquire goods—mostly luxury goods such as ivory, gold, and rare animals—from sub-Saharan Africa; in return, it bartered cloth and other products. Being in the middle of this trade route made it possible for the Nubian kingdom to arrange profitable agreements for resources and products.

However, in ancient times the travel along the Nile that trade required was not easy. In large part, this was due to a series of cataracts, shallow sections of a river over which boats cannot pass. Ethnologist Margaret Shinnie, in *The Horizon History of Africa*, notes, "Although the Nile would appear to be a natural link between the lands and peoples along it banks, river travel [was] made difficult by a series of cataracts or, more properly, rapids."

In ancient times, sailors on the Nile had to rely on slow, troublesome methods of getting around these cataracts. In some cases, they had to take their boats and cargo out of the water and carry them overland. In other cases, they had to walk along the riverbanks, pulling their boats over the rapids with ropes.

A CONFUSING VARIETY OF NAMES

There are six cataracts on the Nile. Since antiquity, they have served as convenient markers to define kingdoms. For example, the kingdom of Kush, one the greatest of the Nubian civilizations, was centered around the Third Cataract.

A word of explanation about the name "Kush" and other proper names from Nubian history is needed. Nubia's overlapping civilizations had many different names, and they were typically called various names by different groups of outsiders. For clarity, in this book "Nubia" generally refers to the region and its people throughout their history, although specific regions and cultures, such as Kush and the Kushites, are identified by name when it is appropriate. (On a related note, various sources and texts spell Nubian proper names in widely different ways. This book uses the most common spellings.)

Another point deserves clarification here: the topsy-turvy distinction between "Upper Nubia" and "Lower Nubia." Upper Nubia is the region closer to the river's headwaters (upstream), while Lower Nubia is the region closer to the mouth of the river (downstream). However, this is very confusing because the Nile flows north. Upper Nubia is south of Lower Nubia.

It is unclear at what point in history the people who lived in this region began to be called Nubians. The name goes back to at least 350 A.D., the date of the first known inscription using that term. However, even this is unclear because this particular inscription can be translated in different ways.

Archaeologists discovered Nubian tombs filled with elaborate artifacts. The beautiful jewelry, pottery, and weapons indicate an advance civilization, but little is known about Nubia's leaders or people.

The meaning and origin of the name "Nubia" are also unclear. One theory that scholars have suggested is that it comes from the Egyptian word *nub*, meaning gold, since in ancient times part of Nubia was a source of that precious metal.

In any case, it is likely that the name is very old. The name of the Kush kingdom is likely even older, as there are many references to it in texts from the earliest times in the region's recorded history. One of these sources is the Bible, which mentions Kush several times. According to these biblical references, the Kushites were descendants of Noah and his oldest son, Kush.

ONLY A FEW CLUES

The Nubians left behind some clues about their culture and civilization. These are artifacts that have been excavated by archaeologists (and, in some cases, grave robbers and adventurers). Among these artifacts are the ruins of burial pyramids and temples, as well as extremely beautiful and surprisingly sophisticated pottery, jewelry, tools, weapons, and other objects. Nubian pottery, to take one example, was, according to many experts, more colorful, intricately decorated, and expertly formed than any other that was produced in the Nile Valley.

Beyond these clues to their culture, frustratingly little is known about the Nubians. The details of their early history were not recorded. The names of only a handful of their kings are known. Little is known about the lives of these royal personages or their subjects. And what chronicles do exist come from outside sources, such as travelers and traders from Egypt, and are not necessarily accurate.

Nonetheless, some facts have emerged about Nubia to trace its earliest days. This story begins in prehistory, when the region's first civilization began to emerge.

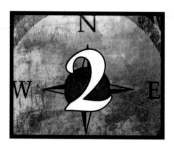

The Earliest Nubians

It is unclear when the first "modern" humans—that is, those clearly showing physically human traits—lived in the region where the ancient civilization of Nubia existed. However, the oldest remains of this type in the world come from Ethiopia, just east of Nubia. These artifacts, two skulls called Omo I and Omo II, are about 195,000 years old. So it is likely that humans also lived in Nubia at about the same time in prehistory.

Few very ancient skeletons have been uncovered in Nubia. No one is certain why this is so. One possible explanation has to do with the way that the region's environment has changed. Nubia was not always a harsh desert. (In fact, archaeologists have found fossilized fish bones and the shells of freshwater creatures there, indicating that it was underwater at some point.) Wetter climates do not preserve bones as well as dry deserts do, so a moist climate in very ancient times could have destroyed such evidence. Furthermore, erosion, especially wind erosion, has been a factor in the disappearance of many traces of these very ancient civilizations.

Fortunately, there are some things that are known about these times. Early settlement sites, dating back roughly 8,000–25,000 years, have been found near the Nile's Second Cataract, just south of the border dividing modern Sudan and Egypt. Some researchers speculate that these may be the earliest known habitats in the entire Nile Valley. The people who lived there were probably originally nomadic, traveling from area to area without a permanent settlement.

However, evidence indicates that they did settle during the Neolithic period (which began in about 9500 B.C., at the end of the Stone Age). They created villages that were both places to live and bases for a variety of food-producing activities. A book prepared by the U.S. Library of Congress, *Sudan: A Country Study*, notes, "By the eighth millennium B.C., people of a Neolithic culture had settled into a sedentary way of life there in fortified mud-brick villages, where they supplemented hunting and fishing on the Nile with grain gathering and cattle herding."

However, these settlements were probably only semipermanent. Evidence indicates that the tribes who lived there had to move periodically. The reasons for this were apparently environmental. The tribes wanted to stay near the Nile, where they could fish and find water for their crops. However, over the course of thousands of years the river's path slowly drifted west. As it did, riverside villages had to be abandoned and new ones established elsewhere.

THE A-GROUP

Around 3800–3100 B.C., the earliest civilization emerged that can be considered genuinely Nubian. (Some scholars think that this culture emerged earlier, about 5000 B.C.) These earliest Nubians lived in Lower (northern) Nubia, along the Nile and between its First and Second Cataracts.

The Nile Valley was an attractive place to live because of its fertile soil. The river flooded every year, and when the floodwaters receded they left behind rich deposits of silt that formed excellent soil for raising crops. This soil, plus water from the Nile and adequate rain, created abundant farmlands. Wheat, barley, and other grains could be grown, and cattle were able to graze in tall grass.

Modern archeologists identify these early Nubians as the "A-Group." As far as is known, the A-Group was the earliest Nubian culture that had strong rulers and could therefore be considered a kingdom. Evidence indicates that several separate A-Group tribes banded together as early as 3300 B.C., roughly around the time the Dynastic period in Egypt began. (The Dynastic period was the period when a series of family dynasties controlled Egypt; it ended about 330 B.C.)

This band may have been only a loosely organized, semi-unified kingdom of tribes, each with its own customs. Archaeology professor Timothy Kendall, in his book *Kerma and the Kingdom of Kush*, writes, "Unlike the Egyptians, the Nubians, in their respective zones and isolated pockets,

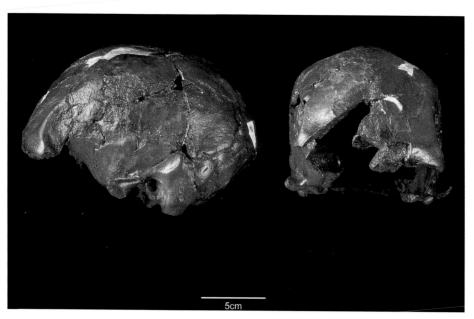

The earliest evidence of modern humans near Nubia was found east of the kingdom in Ethiopia. Omo I and Omo II (*above*) are believed to date back 195,000 years.

were probably united for the most part only on a local scale and probably spoke a variety of different languages or dialects."

The Egyptians had a name for Upper Nubia, the region where these people lived. They called the realm Ta-Seti, a name that roughly translates as "Land of the Bow." It acknowledged the superior hunting skills of the A-Group people—a skill that Nubians would continue to perfect and use for thousands of years against human enemies as well as wild game. Kendall comments, "This reveals what is so well documented in later times: the Nubians were highly skilled archers, and this was a dangerous place to travel without armed escort."

The A-Group apparently had no form of written language. However, evidence clearly shows that its civilization was developing in other ways. This evidence includes pottery, burial tombs, and other artifacts that archaeologists have found. Judging from these recovered objects, the people of Nubia were already in regular contact with the Egyptians. For example, items such as monuments, tools, pottery, and tombs from this era are similar to those associated with Egyptian culture during the same period. Artifacts found at Aswan, at the First Cataract of the Nile, support this theory. Among them are incense burners that are made of local Nubian sandstone but have carvings reminiscent of Egyptian pharaohs.

TRADE BEGINS

The fact that incense burners and other Nubian artifacts were made in styles similar to those of Egypt is an illustration of one of this period's most important developments: the establishment of trade routes through

DID THE A-GROUP CREATE A TOOL FOR ASTRONOMY?

The A-Group was remarkable and mysterious in many ways, but one of the most intriguing things about the culture was the construction of a stone monument in an isolated spot in the desert called Nabta Playa.

There is a theory that this grouping of stones may have been a very early astronomical instrument. It was constructed at some point in the fifth millennium B.C. If it is indeed an astronomical tool, it would predate by some 1,000 years Stonehenge, its famous counterpart in England. Compared to Stonehenge, however, it is very small, only about 13 feet (4 meters) in diameter.

The monument consists of a circle of stones, with four pairs of standing stones inside it. Two of these pairs align to form a line very close to a true north-south line, and the other pairs or gates are along an east-west line. This has been determined by researchers who used global positioning systems to survey the monument very precisely.

The exact purpose of the Nubian monument is unknown, although some researchers think that it was built as a way to determine the arrival of the summer solstice. According to this theory, the standing stones inside the circle would, at a certain point in the year, match up with their counterparts in the constellation Orion.

Nubian territory along the Nile, connecting Egypt with sub-Saharan Africa (south of the desert) as well as regions to the west and east.

There is ample evidence to show that this trade route developed at the same time that the A-Group did. Furthermore, trade goods that came from central Africa have been found in Egyptian tombs dating from this period. These tombs were for Egyptian royalty, and goods from elsewhere were also for them; these products were exotic and valuable, and thus suitable for royal personages. In *A History of Africa*, historian J.D. Fage comments, "As Egypt became richer and produced a specialized ruling class [it needed] foreign trade."

Nubia had little in the way of natural resources that the Egyptians desired. As a result, few goods produced by the A-Group have been uncovered in Egypt. Rather than producing items to trade to the Egyptians, the Nubians instead created a system in which they acted as middlemen, then kept some goods for their own profit. They also acted as toll keepers along the river, receiving items from Egyptian traders in exchange for guaranteeing safe passage through Nubia.

Nubian tribes bartered for a variety of items. From the south came such goods as incense, exotic woods, copper, ivory, gold, shell jewelry, valuable oils, semiprecious stones, and animals such as monkeys, dogs, and giraffes. Gold was available from the east, and carnelian, a gemstone, from the west. Slaves were also an important part of the trade economy, especially pygmies from Africa, who were important to Egyptian religious rituals, perhaps as sacrifices. In exchange for trade goods, Egyptians bartered articles such as agricultural produce, pottery, and clothing.

The A-Group may also have mined iron and other resources of their own for trade to the Egyptians. Charles Bonnet, in an essay in the Wildung book, comments that the A-Group "was perhaps involved in mining resources in the eastern desert."

As the trade for these products increased, so did Nubia's wealth and stability. However, the tribes in the Nubian region did not rely only on trade for their livelihood. To a large degree, they remained what they likely had been for a long time: seminomadic herdsmen.

EGYPT LAUNCHES MILITARY CAMPAIGNS

In many ways the loosely organized tribes in Upper Nubia flourished as a result of their commercial trade with Egypt. But their relationship was a stormy one from the very beginning. Both cultures were generally warlike, and their conflicts sometimes flared into open warfare. Even in times of war, however, the trade route between the two countries generally remained open.

According to inscriptions left by the Egyptians, between 3100 and 2500 B.C., a series of pharaohs organized at least five military campaigns to conquer Lower Nubia. The reason for these forays is unclear, but it is likely that they were triggered by disputes over who controlled the trade route; clearly, it would have been to Egypt's advantage to be the sole power in charge of this lucrative commerce.

This series of invasions was overall unsuccessful, and the various tribes in Nubia remained independent. However, Egypt did have some victories. For example, Senefru, the pharaoh who ruled from about 2575 to 2555 B.C., launched a campaign that brought back considerable treasure—even if it did not subdue the fierce Nubian warriors.

A royal Egyptian report that survives from that operation, quoted in Leslie Greener's book *High Dam Over Nubia*, described one foray as creating "the year of the devastation of the land of the blacks, bringing [back] 7,000 captives, men and women, and 200,000 cattle, sheep, and goats."

The captured people were forced into slavery in Egypt to provide manual labor for royal building projects. The cattle—very valuable items in the economy of the time—were added to the pharaoh's stock of animals. The battle was thus quite successful for the Egyptian ruler. As quoted in Alvin M. Josephy's *Horizon History of Africa*, Nubia scholar P.L. Shinnie comments, "It subdued the local population for some time to come."

A NEW CIVILIZATION EMERGES

This and other campaigns created a drain on the populations of the Nubian tribes. Another phenomenon did as well: when not at war, a steady stream of Nubians migrated northward in search of work. As a result, by about 3100 B.C. the Nubian region was severely underpopulated. The A-Group was dying.

Some researchers believe that they were succeeded by another culture, the B-Group. However, little is known of this culture, apart from the remains of one town where copper was smelted. Some scholars doubt that the B-Group even existed as a separate entity; perhaps, they speculate, it was simply an extension of the A-Group. If it did exist, it was almost certainly small and short-lived. The reasons for this are not understood. One possibility was that warfare and the capture of people for slavery decimated the population.

Another reason may have been changes in climate so severe that they destroyed crops and resulted in serious famine. In *Sudan: Ancient Kingdoms of the Nile*, edited by Dietrich Wildung, archaeologist Charles Bonnet theorized that the demise "may have been caused by a deterioration of climatic [climate-related] and political conditions."

In any case, after a number of years—perhaps centuries—this early culture was replaced by something new: a patchwork of kingdoms that encompassed roughly the same area—Upper Nubia—that the earlier culture had occupied. They were apparently direct descendants of the A-Group. It has been estimated that at its peak about a half million people belonged to this group. Bonnet comments that these people "settled in between the First and Second Cataracts and often occupied the same sites as A-Group, from which they would seem to originate."

THE KINGDOM OF KUSH

Modern archaeologists call this Upper Nubian society the C-Group, but the Egyptians gave a number of different names to the people and the subregions they lived in. At various times, these Egyptian names included Ta Seti, Nehesy, and Yam. However, the most commonly used Egyptian name was Kush. The oldest known Egyptian text that specifically refers to the land as Kush dates from about 1150 B.C., but the civilization was probably well established for centuries before that.

In addition to giving the people of Kush a name, the Egyptians also had a way to describe the region where they lived. According to surviving texts, they found the land a miserable and wretched place in comparison to their own settlements at the mouth of the Nile.

The Egyptians may have considered Kush a wretched place, but it was a desirable location in significant ways. It was centered on a fertile region called the Dongola Reach, above the Third Cataract of the Nile, which was a particularly good location for growing crops and grazing herds of valuable cattle. The reason for the lushness of Dongola was its plentiful supplies of water, which came from the Nile and tributaries feeding into the main river, as well as from rainfall. (This region experienced much more rain in ancient times than it does today.)

The region of Upper Nubia was called Kush, and its capital was Kerma. The remnants of the city have revealed sophisticated tools and architecture, including these 3,500-year-old mud-brick structures located in modern-day Sudan.

KERMA

The political and religious center of Kush was its capital, Kerma. (Kush is sometimes referred to as a whole by this name.) Some evidence indicates that Kerma may have been one of the earliest urban centers in Africa, surprisingly well developed and sophisticated for the time. In the book edited by Wildung, Bonnet comments, "The Classical Kerma period saw the kingdom set up and develop a political and religious system that was apparently very complex."

The remains of Kerma have provided archaeologists with a rich treasure trove of artifacts. This variety of structures, tools, and other relics stands in sharp contrast to the rest of the Kushite kingdom, which apparently was little more than desert land, primitive farming areas, and small, scattered villages.

Among the treasures found in Kerma are the remains of animal pens, defensive walls, a palace complex, workshops for preparing religious offerings, and houses that were probably owned by important people such as nobility and wealthy traders. Also surviving are the ruins of towers. These may have served as lookouts or religious buildings.

All that survive of many of these structures are holes that were dug to support upright beams. However, scientists have been able to put together a fairly complex idea of how they looked. The towers and other buildings were built with tree trunks and mud bricks. Their roofs were cone-shaped and made of palm leaves or fibers. Many buildings were apparently decorated with colorful dyes made from plants. These characteristics are remarkably similar to the style of building that is still used in Sudan today.

Much of what is known about Kerma today comes from a necropolis (burial site) that was created near the ruins of the city. This cemetery is vast: roughly one mile (1.6 km) long and half a mile (0.8 km) wide. It has yielded the remains of approximately 30,000 bodies.

Some, but not all, of the people buried in this place were royalty. Four massive royal tombs have been found there. They are large mounds of earth and stone. The Kushite rulers who were buried there were accompanied in the tombs by servants, apparently sacrificed so that they could help their masters in the afterlife, as well as valuable possessions such as jewelry, weapons, and cattle.

It is not well understood what the Kushite people wore. However, what evidence does exist indicates that men wore loincloths made of goatskins, sometimes with beadwork or designs punched out. Women typically wore leather skirts with beaded or punched designs. Both men and women wore jewelry such as beaded necklaces, and both probably wore sandals made of leather.

Kerma, and Kush as a whole, began a slow decline around 2700 B.C. One probable reason for this, as with earlier settlements, was a change in the course of the Nile. As the river slowly shifted west, the Kushites who depended on it for survival moved as well.

TRADE

Long before it began its decline, the kingdom of Kush had considerable contact with Egypt in the north. A rock inscription discovered south of Aswan describes a meeting between the pharaoh Merenre (who ruled ca.

2255–2246 B.C.) and the chiefs of three kingdoms. This meeting may have taken place because Merenre was intensely interested in building pyramids in his land. For this, he needed to import stone from the south. However, the rapids of the First Cataract prevented any passage of heavy barges laden with stone.

For this reason, the Egyptians apparently approached the leaders of several kingdoms. The Egyptians proposed building canals that would have circumvented the rapids. These canals would have allowed the

Hieroglyphics found in Egyptian tombs indicate that ancient Kushites wore clothes made from animal hides. Leather and goatskin were decorated with punched designs and beads, and citizens accessorized with jewelry and sandals.

Egyptians to quarry stone and bring it north by barge. This proposal was apparently successfully negotiated. The Nubians likely agreed to import wood to build the barges from farther south and probably also negotiated a fee for allowing the Egyptians to pass through their stretch of the river. Weni the Elder, an Egyptian court official, was given the task of overseeing this project. Quoted in an article by Jimmy Dunn on the Web site Tour Egypt, Weni's autobiography states:

> *His majesty sent (me) in order to dig 5 canals in Upper Egypt and in order to build 3 barges and 4 tow-boats of acacia wood of Wawat. [T]he rulers of the Medja hills Irtjet, Wawat, Yam, Medja were cutting the wood for them. (I) did it entirely in one year, floated and loaded with very large granite (blocks) for the pyramid "Merenre-appears-in-splendor." Indeed, I made a saving for the Palace with all these 5 canals.*

Similar negotiations also established the beginnings of a trade route passing from Egypt, through Nubia, and into parts of Africa farther south. This route became much larger and more sophisticated in later centuries.

Much of the information that is known about this route comes from a text written on the tomb of Harkhuf, an Egyptian caravan leader who served Merenre and his successors. According to this document, Harkhuf led four expeditions south, each taking about eight months, to explore the region and make contact with the Nubians. The caravan leader brought gifts from his Egyptian masters and returned home with hundreds of donkeys laden with other gifts.

Quoted in Walter B. Emery's book *Lost Land Emerging* is a letter that Merenre's successor, Pepe II, sent to Harkhuf while the explorer was on one of his journeys. Informed that the trader was returning with a "dancing pygmy" (which may have been a dwarf, not a true pygmy), the young pharaoh wrote back,

> *Come northward to the court immediately, and bring with you the pygmy which you have brought living, in good condition and healthy, from the land of ghosts, for the amusement of the king, to rejoice and gladden his heart. When the pygmy is in the vessel [boat], appoint trustworthy people to be on either side of him. Take care that he does*

not fall in the water. When he is sleeping at night, appoint trustworthy people to sleep beside him in the cabin, and make an inspection ten times a night.

The gradual establishment of trade routes between Egypt through Nubia to the south, in general, provided a reason for contact between the two regions. This contact continued—although with dramatically different result at the time—in the next centuries of Nubia's history.

Shifting Power

During the centuries of Kush's decline, and in the following centuries, the histories of Egypt and Nubia became intimately intertwined. This period of Nubian history roughly corresponds to the period of Egyptian history called the Old Kingdom (ca. 2649–2150 B.C.).

Sometimes the relationship between the two regions was friendly and cooperative, but this was by no means always the case. Rather, they were often at odds with each other over trade and other issues. Generally, whenever Egypt was powerful, it controlled Nubia; when Egyptian power declined, Nubia rebounded in strength. British Egyptologist Walter B. Emery, in his book *Lost Land Emerging*, comments,

> *The Egyptians, representing the highest civilization [in the world] at that time, were pushing south to exploit the gold mines and to trade in ivory, precious wood and other products of Kush. . . . The people of the south, whose culture, we are beginning to realize through recent excavations and research, was by no means negligible, were pushing north to the more fertile parts of the valley of the Nile and the Mediterranean coast.*

The to-and-fro battle was not always equal. For a significant portion of the era, Egypt conquered its neighbor and to a large degree dominated its culture and government. In an article in *National Geographic* magazine, archaeologist William Y. Adams comments, "Between about 1500 B.C. and 1100 B.C., Kush was administered as a province of Egypt."

However, Egypt was never able to pacify Kush entirely, and there were regular flare-ups of rebellion and open violence. Timothy Kendall comments in his book, "When the Egyptians originally started exploring Nubia, which at that point consisted of many different tribes, the people of northern Sudan were very friendly with the Egyptians, and the rulers had good relations with the Egyptian pharaoh. But that didn't last."

On a fairly regular basis, Egypt sent troops south in an effort to conquer the kingdoms there. For example, Sabni, an Egyptian official who governed a portion of Nubia for some time, recorded that he led an army to the region called Wawat. His primary mission was to recover the body of his father, the previous governor, who had been killed while on a trading mission. However, Sabni was also successful in subduing Wawat, splitting it off from the other kingdoms to make sure it remained under Egyptian rule.

In the opinion of Roland Oliver, a British professor of African history, Egypt's efforts to make Nubia a colony, combined with the qualities of the Kushites, helped allow Kush to absorb Egyptian culture and thus develop culturally. Even as late as the first millennium B.C., Oliver writes in his book *The African Experience*, Kush was the only region of Africa other than Egypt itself that had a large enough population and enough organization "to permit the formation of a large state with an element of city-dwellers and a small literate class. This was in the Nilotic [near the Nile] Sudan, and it was partly, though only partly, due to the colonizing activity of Egypt itself."

STAYING SEPARATE

The cultural influence of Egypt might have been strong, but the Kushite kingdom apparently was still able to remain somewhat independent in that regard. Evidence of this includes fragments of pottery produced there, which is unlike the pottery of Egypt of the same period. The Kushite pottery has distinctive red or black coloring and white decoration.

Several other aspects of life in Kush make it clear that it maintained a separate culture. Quoted in the *National Geographic* article, Kendall commented,

> *What's interesting is that . . . the Egyptians let the conquered peoples maintain their own traditions and modes of worship. With Kush*

The pottery of Nubia featured an art style different from that of its ancient neighbors. While Egyptian art focused on religious themes, artisans in Nubia painted dancing cobras and other animals in red, black, and white.

there was much more give and take, and the Egyptians tried to incorporate or combine Nubian religious beliefs with their own. They seem to have combined their own state god, Amun, with the Nubian god and promoted the idea that these two gods were the same. This allowed the pharaohs, who claimed to be the sons of Amun, to claim to be the legitimate rulers of Nubia also.

One interesting cultural phenomenon during this time seems to run counter to any conflict between the regions. It involved large numbers of Nubian warriors choosing to travel northward to join the armies of the pharaohs as mercenaries—that is, paid soldiers. This may have been simply because they recognized that their own land was not powerful enough to stand up to Egypt. Bonnet comments, "[O]ften engaged as mercenaries in the pharaoh's armies, they [the warriors of Nubia] do not however appear to have represented a strong enough force to stand up to the Egyptians."

So many Nubians went to Egypt as mercenaries that by around 2150 B.C. they made up the bulk of Egypt's armies. Many of them settled in Egypt, intermarrying with Egyptian women, and became established citizens of the region. In time, some of their descendents rose high in Egyptian society and played important roles in its government.

THE OLD KINGDOM COLLAPSES

The Egyptian era called the Old Kingdom began to decline around 2134 B.C. This political change had dramatic consequences for Nubia. The collapse of that era's last dynasty had several causes. One involved an ongoing series of conflicts within the Egyptian government; they proved serious enough to cause widespread mismanagement and chaos in the kingdom and the government of its districts.

Another factor was that the realm's treasury was almost empty. The pharaohs of the Old Kingdom had undertaken a series of gigantic building projects, including the Great Pyramid at Giza. These were so expensive that they nearly bankrupted the nation.

And the third reason was the weather; specifically, a devastating dry period. The lack of rain meant that the Nile did not undergo its annual flooding, which the Egyptians relied on for their crops. The resulting famine created serious civil unrest, which in turn resulted in a decline in the power of the pharaohs. In short, life in Egypt was uncertain and chaotic—a far cry from the highly organized structure of past times. Egypt eventually split into two rival states. These two factions waged war against each other, but in about 2050 B.C. the ruling pharaoh in Upper (southern) Egypt, Mentuhotep II, successfully toppled his rival and reunited the land, with the ancient holy city of Thebes as his capital. (This is the site of the modern city of Luxor.) This event marked the beginning of the Middle Kingdom, as the next period of Egyptian history is known. It would last until 1640 B.C. Egypt's Middle Kingdom would soon directly affect the fortunes of Nubia, by becoming far more warlike toward it.

SENUSRET III PUSHES INTO NUBIA

Following the reign of Mentuhotep II, a succession of Middle Kingdom pharaohs, eager to subdue the Nubian tribes, ordered aggressive forays south. Despite fierce opposition from Nubian warriors, Egyptian forces eventually succeeded in penetrating as far as the Second Cataract.

The leader behind this part of the invasion was Senusret III. His goal, to neutralize the threat of aggression from Nubia, was reached in about 1900 B.C. According to Emery in *Lost Land Emerging*, "The real pacification of Nubia was finally accomplished by Senusret III [who] by a series of successful campaigns stamped out any lingering resistance and firmly established the frontiers of Egypt's new dominion, dissipating for many years the haunting menace of Kushite invasion."

Many historians consider Senusret III one of the Middle Kingdom's most powerful rulers. A warrior-king who often personally led his military forces, he headed at least four of the major campaigns sent into Nubia. He also directed a number of major building projects that had military consequences. Notable among these was the repair and improvement of the existing canal through the First Cataract. This project allowed the pharaoh to dramatically extend Egypt's territory, by allowing its ships to journey upriver.

MORE PROTECTION

To protect his newly acquired land, Senusret III built a series of fortresses along 40 miles (64 km) of the Nile River. The northernmost fortress served as a headquarters for the entire route. The southernmost of them marked the boundary between Egyptian territory and southern Africa. They were given names that can be translated into colorful phrases like "Warding off the Bows," "Subduer of the Nehesy [an Egyptian name for the Nubians]," and "Curbing the Foreign Lands."

Ancient Egypt's pharaohs had long coveted Nubia's lands and resources, and conflicts between the two increased at the beginning of the Middle Kingdom. Several pharaohs passed on before Senusret III took power and eliminated any threat of a Kushite takeover.

These forts were close enough to each other that signals could be sent or messengers dispatched with ease. Around each fort was a small town, built along a grid system, and an elaborate defensive system that included massive mud brick walls with openings through which archers could fire. These walls were further surrounded by dry moats. The fortresses were strong enough to hold off even the most aggressive Nubian warriors—at least for the time being.

The forts were not strictly for military use, however; they also had economic value. Their presence ensured that Egypt could protect and control the all-important trade route through Nubia to the south. Shinnie comments, "They served as trading posts as well as military garrisons, for the purpose of Egyptian excursions into Kush was as much for trade as to secure the southern frontier of Egypt."

Senusret was succeeded by his son, Amenemhet III, who reigned for more than four decades. He was not as strong a ruler as his father, however. During Amenemhet III's reign, the power of the pharaonic government began to weaken, and Egypt as a whole began to fracture. Adding to this may have been another serious drought that led to crop failures and resulting civil unrest.

In any case, the overall weakening of Egypt's government meant that its dominance of Nubia also weakened. Egypt was forced to withdraw its forces from there, and by about 1700 B.C., it had completely deserted Nubian territory. The weakness of the Egyptian rulers was further demonstrated when an Asiatic tribe, the Hyksos, invaded Egypt and proceeded to rule there for about a century, circa 1650 to 1550 B.C.

A REVIVED AND INDEPENDENT NUBIA

Taking advantage of this situation, the loose confederacy of Nubia's separate realms stepped in to assert control of the region. In a relatively short time, they banded together more closely and seized the fortresses that the Egyptians had established.

Kerma, the Kushite capital, was by now a well-developed fort and city, with an elaborate defense system that included massive mud and stone walls, projecting watchtowers, and dry ditches that prevented attackers from digging under the walls. Inside these protective walls were temples, homes, a smelter for making metal tools, and manufacturing centers for such goods as pottery.

SENUSRET BOASTS

The Egyptian pharaoh Senusret III had a bold statement carved on a stela (inscribed rock) at Semna, near the Second Cataract of the Nile. This was the point at which he established Egypt's border with Nubia. The inscription was a boast of his prowess as a military leader, a warning to Nubians not to pass north of the inscription, and a warning to his successors to guard this border carefully. It is quoted in Miriam Lichtheim's *Ancient Egyptian Literature: A Book of Readings, Volume I.*

I have made my boundary further south than my father's. I am a king who attacks to conquer, who is swift to succeed. To stop when attacked is to make bold the foe's heart; attack is valor, retreat is cowardice. A coward is he who is driven from his border.

Since the Nubian listens to the word of mouth, to answer him is to make him retreat. Attack him, he will turn his back; retreat, he will start attacking. They are not people one respects; they are wretches, craven-hearted. My Majesty has seen it; it is not an untruth. I have captured their women; I have carried off their dependants, gone to their wells, killed their cattle, cut down their grain, set fire to it. As my father lives for me, I speak the truth!

As for any son of mine who shall maintain this border which My Majesty has made, he is my son, born to My Majesty. But he who abandons it, who fails to fight for it, he is not my son, he was not born to me.

Meanwhile, the Egyptian pharaohs were driving the Hyksos out of their land, a process completed in about 1550 B.C. This marked the beginning of the next period in Egyptian history, the New Kingdom, which lasted until circa 1086 B.C. After regaining their land, the pharaohs wanted to expand their empire, and, not surprisingly, Nubia was the primary target. In the Wildung book, historian Jean Leclant comments, "Scarcely had they rid themselves of the Hyksos when the Egyptians set off to reconquer the south."

The pharaoh Kamose, one of the primary pharaohs in the campaign to defeat the Hyksos, was eager to go to war against Nubia, even though some of his advisors were wary. Quoted in Emery's book, he told them, "I should like to know what serves this strength of mine . . . when I sit between an Asiatic [Hyksos] and a Nubian, each man in possession of his slice of Egypt, and I cannot pass by him as far as Memphis [the ancient city in Lower Egypt]. . . . I will grapple with [my enemy] and slit open his belly."

So Kamose went to war, and soon after he began his campaign he discovered a plot against him. His army captured a messenger heading to the kingdom of Kush from the Hyksos. (These people had retreated to the Middle Eastern desert, except for a small sliver of Egypt in the northeast corner of the Nile Delta, and were eager to attack Egypt again.)

The messenger was carrying explosive news from the king of the Hyksos: he was conspiring to form an alliance with the Kushite king. They would attack Kamose and divide his kingdom. Quoted in Leslie Greener's *High Dam Over Nubia*, the message ran, in part,

> *Have you seen what Egypt has done against me? The ruler there, Kamose . . . is nudging me in my own lands, although I have not attacked him the way he did to you. He has decided to despoil our two lands, mine and yours, and he has caused much damage to them. Come on down river. . . . He is busy with me here, and there is no one to oppose you in Egypt. I will hold him up until you arrive. Then we will divide the towns of Egypt between us and thrive in happiness.*

NUBIA FALLS TO THE EGYPTIANS

Kamose's response to this threat was swift, and it was carried on by his successor, Ahmose I. They decisively drove the Hyksos out of their small part of Egypt and held off any further attacks. This gave the pharaohs complete control again over the whole of Egypt. The victory against the Hyksos inspired Ahmose I and his successors, Amenhotep I and Thutmose I, to follow up with an invasion of Nubia.

These battles were bloodthirsty. In his book, Emery comments that Amenhotep personally slew seven princes of the Hyksos, hanging six on the walls of his capital at Thebes. Of the seventh, an inscription of the time records, "Then the other fallen one was taken upriver to Nubia and hanged on the wall in order to [clearly display] the victories of His Majesty, forever and ever in all lands and countries of the Negro."

BECOMING A COLONY

Eventually, Egypt was able to penetrate deep into the heart of the Kushite kingdom and seize the capital city. Evidence in the form of charred planks indicates that the Egyptian army burned the settlement. The Egyptians then pushed on to the Fourth Cataract, the site of today's Merowe Dam. By circa 1520 B.C., virtually all of northern Nubia had been conquered and

THE PHARAOHS BRAG

The Egyptian pharaohs had no modesty when it came to talking about their exploits on the battlefield or as military commanders. This inscription was carved into a rock at Tombos, just north of Kerma, after the Egyptians had defeated a Nubian army there. Quoted in J.H. Breasted's *Ancient Records of Egypt, Vol. II*, it reads:

> He [Pharaoh Thutmose I] has overthrown the chief of the Nubians. The Nubian is helpless, defenseless in his grasp. He has united the boundaries of his two sides, there is not a remnant of the Curly-Haired who come to attack him; there is not a single survivor among them. The Nubians fall by the sword and are thrust aside in their lands. Their foulness, it floods their valleys. . . . The fragments cut from them are too much for the birds (who eat carrion [dead flesh]).

Another inscription, this one on a rock at the Third Cataract, illuminates how Egyptian forces felt after advancing into Nubian territory despite fierce opposition. Quoted by Leclant in Wildung's book, the text states, "[T]he Nubian archers fallen in carnage are spread over their plains; [Thutmose I] has filled their valleys with their viscera, their blood showers down like rain." The inscription goes on to list names for their Nubian enemies: "the pigtail-wearers," "the scar-bearers," "the [warriors] with burnt faces."

annexed to Egypt. However, pockets of resistance continued to hold out, and the Kushites were not completely subdued until late in the reign of Thutmose III, circa 1480 B.C.

This event marked the beginning of Nubia's days as a true Egyptian colony, not just one country that was heavily dominated by another. Kendall writes, "With the destruction of Kerma and the overthrow of its monarchy, the great Nubian empire . . . came to an end, and its culture was eradicated. For the next four centuries, Kush would become an Egyptian province governed by an Egyptian viceroy."

What had once been the independent kingdom of Kush was now completely a colony. The region's inhabitants previously were subjects of local kings, although they sometimes had to pay a degree of tribute to Egypt; now they toiled only for the benefit of far-off Egyptian nobles and sent a wide variety of goods, produce, and, especially, people northward. In the Wildung book, Leclant comments, "Nubia represented a vast pool of labor: slaves, workers of all kinds, soldiers."

At the same time, increasing numbers of Egyptians migrated south and settled in Nubian territory. They fulfilled a wide variety of trades, government positions, and other lines of work. Kendall comments, "Their numbers must have included artisans, builders, military experts, as well as scribes and accountants."

ADMINISTERING NUBIA

As always, a crucial reason for Egypt to want control of Kush was to keep open the trade route along the Nile to Africa. With the route under Egyptian control, goods passed through with no interference by the Nubians (or money paid to them). Egypt prospered as a result—so much so that it once again became the wealthiest and most powerful nation in the world.

Egypt administered trade and other governmental tasks in Nubia through an elaborate bureaucracy. Overseeing this system was an official who bore a title roughly translatable as "Viceroy of Kush." Collectively, the viceroy and his deputies controlled a region that ranged from Nekhen, about 30 miles (50 km) south of Thebes, to Napata, just below the Fourth Cataract, a distance, by river, of about 700 miles (1,200 km).

Under the viceroy were lesser administrators who controlled individual districts. According to an inscription dating from about 1330 B.C. on the walls of the tomb of one viceroy, Amenhotep Huy, these lesser admin-

After years of fighting and attempted takeovers, Egypt conquered Nubia around 1480 B.C. and turned the kingdom into a colony. Nubian citizens became slaves and laborers to Egypt.

istrators included three "chiefs of Wawat" and six "chiefs of Kush." (These were the names the Egyptians then gave to Upper and Lower Nubia, respectively.)

These lesser bureaucrats were not always Egyptian. Instead, they were often Nubian tribal chiefs the pharaohs considered loyal. But there was little to guarantee that these chiefs would not turn against the Egyptians. As insurance, therefore, the Egyptians routinely brought the sons of the Nubian governors to Egypt. There, the princes were treated well and educated in Egyptian writing, customs, and language. No matter how these young men were treated, however, they remained essentially hostages; their presence in Egypt ensured the loyalty of their fathers to the pharaoh.

Perhaps the primary duty of the Nubian bureaucracy was to collect taxes. The viceroy arranged for these tributes to be sent north, typically in the form of goods such as gold, cattle, agricultural produce, and slaves.

The viceroy presented these treasures to the king in elaborate ceremonies. A surviving inscription describes one such tribute as including so much ebony wood that it took a hundred men to carry it. Another example, found in the tomb of the pharaoh Tutankhamen, is a painting of a tribute ceremony that shows dark brown and copper-colored Nubians bringing a variety of treasures, such as platters overflowing with gold rings and giraffes on leashes.

The viceroy and his administrators were also responsible for overseeing a provincial army. This military force was made up of a variety of soldiers: Egyptians, Nubians, and outside mercenaries. Nubia also continued to supply troops to Egyptian armies stationed in the north. A number of wall carvings and written records, for example, reveal the use of Nubian troops to defend Egypt's northern borders. Some Nubian warriors were highly prized for their skills; for example, men from the Medjay tribe served as elite scouts and protectors of royal and religious complexes.

ASSIMILATING INTO EGYPTIAN LIFE

As people increasingly moved back and forth across the border for trade, military service, or other reasons, Nubia began to change. Increasingly, it adopted Egyptian religion, culture, and customs. In fact, Nubians and Egyptians grew so closely related during this period that some scholars consider the two groups virtually indistinguishable.

Egypt's leaders actively fostered this mingling of cultures. They wanted to encourage Egyptians to emigrate to what was considered an alien and inhospitable land, a place where few Egyptians would willingly live or die. (Dying was especially important, given the need to prepare for a good afterlife.) In the Wildung book, Leclant quotes a saying of the time: "If I lie, may my ears and nose be cut off—or let me be sent to Kush."

But the pharaohs realized that one way to encourage resettlement was to emphasize the interconnectedness of the two regions. They went even farther, planting the idea that, indeed, Nubia had always been a part of Egypt. And so a number of aspects of Egyptian culture made their way south.

For example, Nubian burial practices became increasingly similar to those of Egypt, with royalty entombed in pyramids. Schools to teach

Egyptian ways were established for the children of Kushite nobility. Kings and other members of this nobility gave themselves Egyptian titles.

MERGING THE RELIGIONS

Religion was an especially important element in merging the cultures. Little is known of the religious beliefs of Nubia before the Egyptian occupation, although evidence indicates that, like the Egyptians, they had multiple gods, practiced sun worship, and believed that their king was a direct descendant of the sun. There were some differences, however; notably, the Nubians worshipped a lion warrior god, Apedemak, a practice that probably originated with cultures in tropical Africa. Apedemak was usually shown wearing armor and sitting on a throne or war elephant, holding weapons and ropes that restrained prisoners, elephants, or lions.

All in all, the similarities outweighed the differences, so it is likely that merging the two religions was relatively easy. To facilitate this, major temples dedicated to Amun, the Egyptian sun god, were built in Nubia. The most elaborate of these, at Napata (now Jebel Barkal), stood at the foot of a small sandstone butte. This outcropping was said to be Amun's home because from one angle it looks like a rearing cobra, the symbol used on the royal Egyptian crown. The pharaohs considered the site so sacred that it became the location for their coronation ceremonies.

For a time, the Egyptian royalty's strategy worked. Many of their subjects willingly moved south, settled, and intermarried with Nubians. However, the mingling of cultures did not prove strong enough. Following the death of an important Egyptian pharaoh, Ramses II, circa 1224 B.C., Egypt again fell into political disarray and split in two. Pharaohs continued to govern Lower (northern) Egypt, but Upper Egypt was governed by a succession of priests of the sun god.

As unity in Egypt dissolved, so did Egyptian control over Nubia. By about 1080 B.C., Egypt's army had essentially withdrawn from the region. Nubian kings who had once served as Egyptian representatives now assumed command. They separated Nubia from its former master. In *A History of Africa*, J.D. Fage remarks, "Egyptian control of Nubia faltered, and out of the viceroyalty an independent kingdom emerged. . . . For a space, the power of organized government in Kush was greater than it was in Egypt."

At first, this organization was not able to sustain itself. Rule fell apart and much of Lower Nubia became a sparsely populated no-man's-land ruled by several warring groups. Remnants of Egyptian occupation, such as temple sites and urban centers, fell into ruin. The trade route apparently dried up as well. No surviving texts mention African products making their way north until about 950 B.C., when it was recorded that the pharaoh sent gifts that had come from Africa to kings in what is now Iraq.

Fortunately, the situation in Lower Nubia did not last long. The Kushites were able to reunite the region into a single, centrally controlled kingdom with its capital at Napata. This process of creating a single, strong government apparently was complete by the mid-700s B.C. At this point, Nubia was ready to invert the events of previous centuries.

Once, it had been a province of Egypt. Now, as a result of Egypt's political disarray, Nubia was about to become one of the greatest realms in Africa's long history, perhaps even one of the greatest in all of world history. In the Wildung book, Kendall asserts, "Of the great states spawned by the Middle Nile, none appears so mysteriously or unexpectedly in history, none had such an explosive impact on the world stage, none acquired such a vast empire, and none endured so long as that which emerged in the eighth century B.C." The next period in Nubia's history was undoubtedly its greatest.

The Meroitic Era: Nubia's Golden Age

When Nubia set out to occupy Egypt, a king named Alara, followed by his son Kashta, led the way. These rulers considered themselves the rightful heirs to the Egyptian throne; Kashta even gave himself the (somewhat premature) title of "King of Upper and Lower Egypt," thus putting himself on an equal plane with the pharaohs.

Kashta is considered by many to be the founder of the Twenty-fifth Dynasty, the "Nubian Dynasty" during which pharaohs of Nubian descent ruled the entire realm. (This era is sometimes called the Napatan Era, after Nubia's capital at the time.)

However, Kashta was not successful in completely subduing both Lower and Upper Egypt. That was completed by his son Piye, who reigned circa 728–706 B.C. While warring against Egypt, Piye inspired his people by promoting the belief that Nubia and Egypt had once been a single empire and should unite again. This was a reversal of the same tactic that the pharaohs had earlier used, urging their subjects to invade and settle in Nubia. To bolster his argument, Piye announced that he was the reincarnation of Thutmose III, Nubia's conqueror.

The war the Nubian leader waged was not an easy victory. Piye faced an especially difficult campaign to overcome a band of small kingdoms in the northeastern part of Egypt. They managed to slow Piye's advance, but by the last part of the eighth century B.C. the Nubians decisively controlled all of Egypt.

Piye solidified his power there by naming his sister, Amenirdis I, to a powerful position: the symbolic "divine wife" of Amun, the sun god, at the main Egyptian temple of Karnak in Thebes. Tradition held that this role made her both a divine being and a mortal ruler over the area around Thebes. Together, she and her brother now had absolute control over virtually the entire Nile Valley.

PIYE THE PIOUS

Records of Piye's rule were no doubt biased in favor of him, praising him. According to these inscriptions, Piye was a highly competent and compassionate ruler. The records assert that he tried to avoid bloodshed when possible, forgave his enemies, and was pious in his devotion to the gods.

Whether or not these assessments are accurate, it does appear that he was not greedy. Although he could easily have done so, evidence indicates that he had no interest in rule directly over northern Egypt. Instead, he was content to remain in Napata, rebuilding the ruined Egyptian temples, and to control through deputies important points such as Thebes and the oases of the western desert.

Piye's dedication to the ancient gods of Egypt can be seen in the following excerpt, quoted in Miriam Lichtheim's *Ancient Egyptian Literature: A Book of Readings, Vol. II*. It is from a stela detailing one of Piye's victories. It instructs his royal troops on how to behave at the great temple of Amun at Thebes:

> *Then his majesty sent an army to Egypt and charged them strictly: When you have reached Thebes at Karnak Temple, go into the water. Cleanse yourselves in the river; wear the best linen. Rest the bow; loosen the arrow. Boast not to the lord of might (i.e. Amun), for the brave has no might without him. He makes the weak-armed strong-armed, so that many may lie before the few, and a single one conquers a thousand men! Sprinkle yourselves with water of his altars; kiss the earth before his face.*

AFTER PIYE

When Piye died, he was buried beside his ancestors at el-Kurru, southwest of Jebel Barkal, under a small, Nubian-style pyramid. In accordance with the custom of the time, tombs for his wives and horses surrounded his body. (His sister, the royal priestess, was buried at a site called Medinet Habu.) Piye's successor was his brother Shabaqo. Shabaqo's main contribution to Nubian history was to move the capital city from Napata north to Memphis, at the mouth of the Nile Delta. From then on, he and his dynastic successors took up permanent residence there.

During this dynasty's reign, Piye and his successors maintained some elements of their Nubian heritage. However, over time they became increasingly "Egyptianized." In large part, this was because they did not consider themselves foreigners; rather, they thought of themselves—as Piye had asserted—as legitimate rulers of what had once been a single empire under the protection of the sun god.

The succession of Nubian pharaohs thus adopted the titles, names, religious rituals, manners, and customs of earlier and presumably purer Egyptian rulers. For example, Shabaqo ordered that his burial site be an Egyptian-style pyramid, despite the fact that Egyptians had long before stopped building them. Furthermore, the Nubian rulers of Egypt directed their royal artisans to use artistic styles from the Old and Middle Kingdoms, styles that had long before fallen out of fashion. Another way in which these rulers adopted Egyptian customs was that they apparently lived in Lower Egypt permanently, traveling to their ancestral homeland only to be buried.

On the other hand, evidence indicates that the people of Nubia, to the south and thus far removed from the royal court, were less "Egyptianized" than their rulers. It appears, in general, that they instead maintained the old ways and customs of traditional Nubian culture. In his book *Africa in History*, scholar Basil Davidson writes, "Kushite pharaohs ruled Upper Egypt for a century, and the whole of Egypt for more than fifty years; yet the impact of all this on their homeland seems to have been remote and even insignificant. Their own peoples continued to live as they had lived before."

TAHARQA

One of Piye's successors, his son Taharqa, is considered to be the most significant of the Nubian pharaohs after his father. As a young man, Taharqa had a distinguished military career. He became ruler at the age of about 32 and remained on the throne for 26 years.

Taharqa did much to maintain and expand the Nubian empire. Among other accomplishments, he won significant victories over a number of desert peoples who lived to the east and west of the Nile Valley, gained firm control of the valuable western oases, erected new temples and created new towns across his kingdom, and strengthened Egyptian naval power by seizing Phoenician port cities and fleets of ships. (Phoenicia, in modern-day Lebanon, Syria, and Israel, was renowned for its sailing vessels and ports.)

However, Taharqa was unsuccessful in the most important area of all: maintaining the empire. Unable to fend off invasions from Assyria (now Iraq), he lost his kingdom to them. The Assyrians, who were superb warriors, had advanced steadily from the east and by the mid-600s B.C. controlled crucial Middle Eastern regions that had once been Taharqa's allies. The Assyrians then mounted regular attacks on Egypt, attempting invasions almost annually.

In 669 B.C., they succeeded in their quest and forced Taharqa out of Memphis. He had to flee south and reinstate the former Nubian capital of Napata. Taharqa's defeat was a devastating and humiliating blow. The once-powerful Taharqa lost almost everything: his chief wife and sons, his capital city, the lands of Upper and Lower Egypt, and all of his treasure. Within five years, the former pharaoh was dead.

AN END—AND A BEGINNING

However, the era of Nubian control over Egypt was not completely over. Taharqa's nephew Tanutaman succeeded him and was able to retake Egypt in 663 B.C., forcing the new rulers out. The victory was short-lived, however; the Assyrian army attacked again in 656 B.C. and forced Tanutaman back to Napata. This defeat marked the definitive end of Nubia's reign over Egypt, although the leaders of Nubia continued to consider themselves the legitimate rulers.

Napata did not remain the Nubian capital for long. The new ruler of Egypt, Psammeticus II, marched his army south to the region between the Third and Fourth Cataracts and sacked the city in about 593 B.C.. The Nubians—probably led at this point by a ruler named Aspelta—were forced to once again retreat, and this time they relocated their capital to Meroe. (This name is often used for both the region and the city.) It proved to be a fortuitous move. The next period in history—the Meroitic Era—is widely regarded as the Golden Age of Nubian culture, an era of unparalleled wealth and stability.

There were several reasons why the city of Meroe was a good choice. For one thing, it was at a major point along the river's trade route: the confluence of the White and Blue Niles, two rivers that join as they flow northward to become the main Nile River. This was the junction of several river and caravan routes connecting central Africa to Egypt and, to the east, the Red Sea and Ethiopia. The Nubians were thus in a position to prosper from barter and trade.

The area around the city of Meroe, located as it was between two rivers, offered the Nubians many other advantages. It was relatively secure compared to Napata. It was also close to sources of two important natural resources: hardwood (for making charcoal) and iron. The charcoal was used in furnaces that turned iron ore into metal suitable for making arrowheads and spears. The iron industry was increasingly crucial for military purposes, as history professor Toyin Falola notes in his book *Key Events in African History*: "The Nubians knew that the security of their

The Kushite leader Piye conquered northern territories during a time of political confusion in Lower Egypt and created one large kingdom that encompassed all of Egypt and Nubia. His son, Taharqa (*above, with falcon god Hemen*), further expanded this territory as pharaoh.

kingdom now depended on building an iron industry. . . . [And so] the potential for the economy was enormous."

Furthermore, the land of Meroe was fertile. The soil was good because of the silt left by the annual river floods; there was also ample water for livestock and for staple crops such as millet and barley. Writer John Reader, in his book *Africa: A Biography of the Continent*, comments,

> *With extensive rain-fed agriculture, and grasslands to east and west supporting herds of cattle and other livestock, Meroe was founded on a robust mixed-farming economy. Add to this the fortuity [good luck] of access to the Red Sea and to the resources of the African hinterland at a time when rising Greek and Roman prosperity had created a demand for exotic goods, and the wealth and power of Meroe at its height during the last few centuries BC is not at all surprising.*

IMPROVING THE NEW CAPITAL

Once Meroe was established as the new capital, the Meroites—as they became known—added to and improved the already existing city. For example, they built large artificial lakes that were used to hold rainfall for future use. Stone statues of guardian lions and frogs apparently were erected around many of these artificial lakes, perhaps to protect their contents.

The Meroites also constructed many new religious sites. Among these was the spectacular "Great Enclosure," a collection of courtyards and about 20 temples in the city. They were dedicated to both Egyptian and Kushite gods, surrounded by high stone walls and connected by corridors and ramps.

The city of Meroe was the capital, but it was not the only important urban center. The ruins of several other sites have also been found; most are close to the Nile, while some are as far as 60 miles (96 km) away from the river. One of these urban centers was the ancient walled town of Jebel Barkal. This was also the site of the sacred mountain that had long been the place where Kushite kings were crowned and where a number of them were buried as well.

During this period of rebirth for the Nubians, they began to move away from the customs and practices they had borrowed for centuries from Egypt. In their place came more distinctive and individual forms

AFTER THE INVASION

The following passage is part of an inscription written by Assurbani-pal, king of Assyria, after his successful invasion of Egypt and Kush in 664–661 B.C. It is quoted in D.D. Luckenbill's *Ancient Records of Assyria and Babylonia, Vol. II*:

> Tarku [i.e. Taharqa], king of Egypt and Kush, heard of the advance of my army and mustered his fighting men against me, offering armed resistance and battle. With the help of Assur, Bel, Nabu, the great gods, my lords, who advance at my side, I defeated his army in a battle on the open plain. Tarku heard of the defeat of his armies, while in Memphis. The terrible splendor of Assur and Ishtar overcame him and he went mad. He forsook Memphis and fled to save his life. The terror of the weapon of Assur, my lord, overwhelmed him and the night of death overtook him. Thereupon, Tandemane [Tanutaman] seated himself upon his royal throne. Thebes and Heliopolis he made his strongholds. He gathered together his forces.
>
> A swift messenger came to Nineveh and told me thereof. I made straight for Egypt and Kush. Tandamane heard of the advance and that I was invading Egypt. He forsook Memphis and fled to Thebes to save his life. The kings, prefects, governors, whom I had installed in Egypt, came to meet me and kissed my feet.
>
> I took the road after Tandamane, marched as far as Thebes, his stronghold. He saw the approach of my terrible battle array, forsook Thebes, and fled [so that] Thebes [by] my hands [was] captured in its entirety. Silver, gold, precious stones, the goods of his palace, all there was, brightly colored and linen garments, great horses, the people, male and female, two tall obelisks, made of shining electrum, whose weight was 2500 talents and which stood by the gate of the temple, I removed from their positions and carried them off to Assyria. Heavy plunder . . . I carried away from Thebes. With a full hand I returned in safety to Nineveh, my royal city.

of Nubian culture. For example, on pottery and other works of art, royalty was depicted as looking much more "African," with dark skin, curly hair, and distinctive clothing and crowns—a far cry from the Egyptian-style portraits that had been in favor for so long. Furthermore, Egyptian hieroglyphs for writing were largely abandoned. In their place, a new and distinctly Nubian script emerged: a form of writing that used an alphabet of 23 characters.

NO MORE ROYAL SUICIDES

Evidence indicates that the Nubian rulers during this period did not appear in public or interact with their subjects often. Instead, they preferred to seclude themselves in their palaces, leaving their generals to battle the Assyrians, nomadic desert tribes, and other enemies. Some historians speculate that the only times kings ventured beyond their palaces were for official visits such as religious ceremonies held at Nubian temples.

There were apparently some unusual aspects to royal life during this period. For example, according to Diodorus Siculus, a Greek historian of the first century B.C., the highest priests had the power to name a king. Not only that, they also had the power to send a message—supposedly directly from the sun god Amun—advising the king that his rule was over. According to tradition, the king would then commit suicide.

This practice apparently ended when one king, Ergamenes, ignored this command. Not only did he refuse to kill himself, he also ordered the deaths of the priests. Ergamenes thus overrode the mighty power of the priests and asserted his royal right to control the Nubian people. Quoted in an anonymous article on the Web site NubiNet (www.nubianet.org), a Greek historian of the time wrote, "With the determination worthy of a king he came with an armed force to the forbidden place where the golden temple . . . was situated and slaughtered all the priests, abolished this tradition, and instituted practices at his own discretion."

As power shifted from the priests to the kings of Nubia, the realm's relationship with Egypt also changed. Ergamenes and other rulers maintained generally peaceful and close relationships with their Egyptian counterparts. These pharaohs comprised the Ptolemaic dynasty, which had it roots in Greece. As the Egyptian rulers' contact with Nubia expanded, Greek culture began to spread southward. This grew to the point where

After losing the territories of Egypt, the Nubian kingdom relocated to Meroe and rebuilt its civilization around agriculture and metalwork. One of the city's greatest sites, the Great Enclosure, features lion statues and temples dedicated to both Egyptian gods and the sons of a Nubian leader.

the characteristics of some Nubian gods began to take on those of Grecian gods. According to the Roman historian Pliny the Elder, writing in the first century A.D., a significant number of Greeks lived in Meroe during this period. Numerous Greek objects excavated at Meroe, such as a vase made in Athens, support Pliny's statement and the existence of a continuing trade route.

WHAT THE MEROITES ATE

During this period, a number of travelers from outside came through Meroitic Nubia and recorded what they saw. Among them was a Greek geographer, Strabo. He noted that the people there lived primarily on millet and barley, from which they also brewed an alcoholic drink, as well as meat, animal blood, milk, and cheese.

However, he stated, the Meroites had no fruit trees except for a few date palms in the royal palaces. Furthermore, he said, poor people sometimes had to survive on grass, soft twigs, and water lilies from the river. Quoted in Tomas Hagg's *Textual Sources for the History of the Middle Nile Region Between the 8th Century BC and 6th Century AD, Vol. III,* Strabo also noted other customs:

> *They appoint as kings those who are distinguished by beauty or skill in cattle-breeding or courage or wealth. The Aithiopians [as the Greeks called them] also have the following custom. If a king is mutilated in any part of his body, whatever the circumstances, those who are together with him suffer the same thing, and they even die with him. Therefore they guard their king scrupulously.*

The Greeks were by no means the only foreigners to become curious about—and influence—Nubia. The mighty Roman Empire also entered the scene at this point, ushering in a new phase of Nubian history.

The Post-Meroitic Era

At its peak, the mighty Roman Empire sprawled across most of Europe, Asia Minor, and North Africa. It took control of Egypt in the first century B.C. The Roman nobleman Octavian, who was called Augustus Caesar after being crowned emperor, led this conquest following the deaths of his rival, Mark Antony, and Antony's lover, Egypt's legendary Queen Cleopatra VII.

THE ROMANS AND THE MEROITES

Once established in Egypt, the Romans made a number of expeditions to explore the region to the south. One mission the Romans undertook was an expedition to find the source of the Nile. Quoted in Josephy's book, Pliny reported that this mission observed that "the grass in the vicinity of Meroe becomes of a greener and fresher color [than further north], and there is some slight appearance of forests, as also traces of rhinoceros and elephant."

This description, made some time after the expedition, was probably accurate. On the other hand, Pliny also repeated reports that some of the Nubian people had no noses, that others had no upper lips, and that still others had no tongues or had mouths that had grown together. His chronicle, clearly, must be taken with a grain of salt.

At first, not surprisingly, the Meroites were decidedly hostile toward the Romans. In 24 B.C., six years after the start of the Roman occupation of Egypt, the Meroites marched north against the new rulers. They advanced through Lower Nubia as far as Aswan, crossed the border, and mocked the Romans by seizing statues of Augustus that had been erected there.

Among the artifacts archaeologists have since discovered to support this disdain is a bronze head of Augustus. It had been buried beneath steps at the front of a temple in Meroe; anyone entering the building would step on the bust as a sign of disrespect.

WAR AND PEACE

The Romans quickly retaliated. An army led by a distinguished general, Gaius Petronius (also called Publius Petronius), was sent south. Petronius succeeded in penetrating deep into Meroe and, among other things, he destroyed the city of Napata. Several years of war followed, until the two sides were able to forge a peace treaty in 20 B.C.

The terms of the treaty generally favored the Meroites. The Romans agreed to withdraw from a significant amount of Nubian land. Furthermore, the Meroites did not have to pay tribute to the Roman emperor, something the Romans had desired. However, the Nubians agreed to let the Romans maintain a portion of land, called the Dodekashoinos ("Twelve-Mile Strip"), as a military border zone. This peace treaty held up for a long time afterward—roughly three centuries, well into the glory days of the Roman Empire.

The end of conflict with Rome led to a number of cooperative efforts between the former enemies. For example, together they constructed a magnificent building, the Temple of Dendur. The sandstone walls of this temple were adorned with, among other decorations, Egyptian hieroglyphic writing in which Augustus (appearing as a pharaoh) pays homage to three Nubian gods and two recently deceased young men who, it is believed, were the sons of a Meroite ruler.

The end of conflict and the establishment of a clear border also allowed the Meroites to sustain their economy. As a result, Meroe enjoyed a period of widespread order and prosperity. The remains of large, spacious houses that have since been discovered are an indication of this prosperity. Trade remained important, and Meroe remained a center for the production of such goods as pottery, baskets, cloth, leather goods, and metal tools and weapons. Still another part of the Nubian economy was the gold mined in the Red Sea Hills to the east.

After their conflict ended, former enemies Rome and Nubia came together to build the Temple of Dendur. The temple was commissioned by Roman emperor Augustus and is now exhibited in New York City's Metropolitan Museum of Art (*above*).

However, agriculture remained the region's primary activity. Small plots of well-irrigated land lined the banks of the Nile, and farmers continued to grow abundant crops of such staples as barley, millet, and dates. These farmers were able to greatly increase their productivity, in large part because of a radical agricultural innovation: the oxen-powered waterwheel. Introduced by the Romans, this revolutionary machinery gave farmers the ability to irrigate even the fields that were high above the level of the river.

THE KANDAKES

During this period of prosperity, there was an unusual tradition for the time: a number of rulers were women. According to Roman historians, a one-eyed queen ruled the Meroites through the time of war and the peace agreement with the Romans. This one-eyed queen was probably one of two leaders, either Amanirenas or Amanishakheto (sources differ).

The Meroite queens held the title *kandake* or *kentake*. (The modern name Candice, or Candace, derives from the Greek version of this ancient word.) Nearly a dozen kandakes have been identified to date. Among them were Shanakdakheto, Amanitore, and Lahideamani. The New Testament of the Bible refers to a kandake, calling her the "Queen of Ethiopia."

The kandake about whom archaeologists know the most is Amanishakheto, who probably reigned from about 10 B.C. to 1 A.D. Queen Amanishakheto established her capital at Wad Ban Naga, a river port. The ruins of a palace for the queen, two stories high and made of mud brick, and several stone temples still exist there, as does evidence of a cemetery and surrounding farmland. However, Amanishakheto was not buried at her capital but in the royal cemetery at Meroe.

Some queens apparently ruled alone, while others may have co-ruled with their husbands. They may also have been the mothers of princes too young to rule themselves. Quoted in "The Meroitic State," an anonymous article on Nubianet.org, the sixth-century historian Oecumenius noted, "Candace is what the Aithiopians call every mother of a king. [Her son] is traditionally regarded as a son of the sun god."

Carvings of kandakes found on the walls of tombs and temples portray them as large people, probably to indicate their importance, but also to emphasize that they were noble and thus well fed and healthy. The kandakes were apparently fierce warriors; wall carvings dating to about 170 B.C. reveal Shanakdakheto dressed in armor and wielding a spear in battle. Other portraits depict kandakes wearing elaborate clothing and jewels, as well as the ritual facial scars favored by Meroitic royalty.

THE POST-MEROITIC PERIOD

Despite the strong presence of the kandakes and other rulers, however, in time the prosperous Meroite kingdom began to decline. In the next centuries, Nubia's distinctive culture was fated to disappear. In its place emerged a post-Meroitic culture that lasted from roughly 350 to 650 A.D. and was dominated by tribes invading from outside the kingdom.

The reasons for this fundamental shift—the decline of the Meroitic empire—are not well understood, although there are several plausible theories. One concerns the devastating costs of environmental damage. Evidence indicates that the Meroites practiced agricultural techniques

Romans hired Noubadians and members of other tribes as mercenaries to eliminate their enemies. People from different parts of the world, like the Noubadians, were often depicted on Roman urns (*above*).

that directly resulted in destruction of the land. For example, the Meroites apparently overgrazed the land with their cattle. This resulted in a lack of vegetation, which in turn caused serious erosion of the soil. The destruction went further when the lack of fertile soil resulted in an increasing inability to raise enough crops to support the population.

Even before the emergence of any other factors that may have figured in the kingdom's decline, it is likely that this environmental degradation already made the collapse of the Meroitic kingdom inevitable. In his book *Africa: A Biography of the Continent*, Reader comments, "Trees to fuel iron-smelting furnaces had been felled faster than new ones could grow. Deforestation led to erosion and a loss of topsoil. A region which had supported thriving agricultural populations for a thousand years could be farmed no longer."

LOSING THE TRADE ROUTE

The damage caused by environmental mismanagement had wide implications in other areas of life, notably the kingdom's economy. As it became more difficult to find wood to fuel furnaces to make iron, Meroitic ironworks began to close down. This, of course, resulted in a shortage of iron weapons and tools. These prized objects were, in turn, not available either for domestic use or as goods for barter.

These iron tools and weapons had been the primary items that Meroites made themselves that were valuable trade products. When they were no longer available, merchants and traders from other regions began to frequent Meroe less, and the kingdom no longer held a position as a major trading civilization. Traders from other regions even began to avoid using routes that passed through Meroe. Instead, they increasingly favored a new route that was opening between southern Africa and the Middle East. This new route passed through the neighboring kingdom of Axum, east of Meroe on the Red Sea (and now part of northern Ethiopia).

The drop in trade was a serious blow, but it was not the only reason for Meroe's slow decline. Increasingly, the kingdom was the target of raids from powerful outside raiders. These nomadic desert tribes regularly attacked Meroitic settlements on the edges of the kingdom and were highly successful, in part, because they had mastered an important tool of warfare: the ability to breed and ride horses and camels.

WHAT THE AITHIOPIANS DID

A Greek observer, Nicolaus of Damascus, describes in this passage, from the late first century B.C., a few of his observations about the "Aithiopians," as the Greeks called the Nubians:

Aithiopians have a particular respect for their sisters; the kings do not leave the succession to their own but to their sisters' sons. When there is no successor, they choose as king the most handsome of all and most warlike. They cultivate piety and righteousness. Their houses have no doors; and although there are many things left lying in the streets, no one ever steals them.

The use of these animals was not new, but the nomadic tribes had developed this aspect of battle to a very high level. It was a vitally important element of war because a soldier attacking while mounted on an animal was far more effective than a warrior who was on foot. (This was also true for mounted soldiers elsewhere during this period, such as warriors in Europe and China.) Furthermore, the speed of the nomad's camels gave the warriors increased maneuverability; they could carry out small, fast, and effective surprise attacks, then quickly retreat in what was, essentially, a form of guerrilla warfare. All in all, the desert nomads were formidable enemies. Roland Oliver comments that they "were known and feared for their swift-moving cavalry forces, armed with bows as well as swords, and equipped with the earliest bits, bridles, and spurs to be used anywhere in Africa."

THE BLEMMYES AND THE NOUBADIANS

As is true for other periods of Nubian history, precious little is known about this era, since few records or artifacts have survived. However, it appears that several of these outside tribes eventually settled in parts of the Meroitic kingdom, forming a collective culture that archaeologists call the X-Group, or Ballana culture. By the late third century A.D., the descendants of some of these invading tribes dominated the region.

Although the details are unclear, it appears that these people had frequent contact with the Roman Empire. In large part, this contact was through trade. This aspect of their interactions is evident because Roman artifacts from this time, such as vessels made of bronze and glass and medallions with portraits of Roman emperors, have been found in Meroe.

There were many formerly nomadic tribes that settled in Nubia during this period, but the most prominent were the Noubadians (or Noba) and the Blemmyes (Beja). The Noubadians originally came from the oases of the western Egyptian desert and had settled near what is now the Sudanese-Egyptian border. The Blemmyes, meanwhile, came from east of the Nile, probably the hills near the Red Sea, before they established themselves in the region south of Aswan.

Both groups had adopted a number of customs from surrounding cultures, including the use of Greek writing (from the Byzantine Empire) and, from Egypt, symbols associated with pharaohs and the worship of their ancient gods. Despite having such cultural traits in common, however,

Meorite queens were called kandake, and one of the most famous kandakes was a one-eyed queen who ruled during the peace truce with the Romans. Above, this gold bracelet belonged to the queen and was found in her tomb.

relations between them were often hostile. On at least one occasion the Romans hired one tribe as mercenaries to fight the other. In this instance, surviving Roman records state that in 297 A.D. the Roman emperor Diocletian recruited the Noubadians to help him defend the frontier of his empire from the Blemmyes.

THE AXUMITES

At some point in the fourth century, another group of warriors from outside the region entered Nubian history. These were the Axumites. Axum (also spelled Aksum) was a nation east of Nubia that, at its peak, encompassed large portions of what are now Ethiopia, Yemen, Saudi Arabia, and Eritrea.

These people were led into Nubia by the greatest Axumite king, Ezana, in about 350 A.D. Evidence of this includes an inscription in the Axumite's king's language, Ge'ez, that was found in the region. This document indicates that Ezana's military campaign reached as far as the Fifth and Sixth Cataracts. It is unclear whether or not Axum succeeded in conquering the entire region, however.

As was so often the case, Ezana's purpose in invading Nubia was, in large part, economic—specifically, to gain complete control over the flow of goods between Africa and the lands to the east, such as Arabia and India. He already had partial control, since some of the route passed through Axum. Ezana's kingdom was already well situated for trade, in highlands near the Red Sea that were directly on the main trade routes. Now, by annexing a good part (or perhaps all) of Nubia, the Axumite king controlled nearly all of this important trade route.

Trade was strong, Axum became fabulously wealthy, and Ezana and his successors dominated post-Meroitic Nubia for centuries. However, the region did not remain static; rather, it continued to evolve in significant ways. One of the most significant was the conversion of the realm to Christianity, which took deep root in Nubia. The other was the gradual lessening of Axum's control of Nubia. The convergence of these changes would shape the region's future for hundreds of years.

Nubia's Christian Era

Evidence points to Axumite control over Nubia very gradually beginning to loosen after about a century. The reasons for this are unclear; however, it is likely that it was connected to the general decline experienced by the kingdom of Axum, as military aggression from enemies in the Middle East eroded its power.

As the control of Axum over its territory slipped away, the Nubian population was able to assert itself, allowing them to create an independent political structure. This eventually took the form of three loosely allied kingdoms: Nobatia (in the north, bordering Egypt); Makuria (in the central part of the region); and Alodia (the southernmost realm).

MAKURIA

In general, what little information exists about these kingdoms is sketchy or contradictory. Virtually all of this information comes from accounts by Arab travelers and traders of the period who passed through Nubia. Such chronicles cannot be guaranteed to be reliable, however, since these observers were not always sympathetic to the Nubians.

Because so little information has been uncovered, and because some of it is contradictory, there are no known details about the early development of these kingdoms as distinct entities. Nor is detailed information available about the ways in which their governments were structured. For example, some surviving documents indicate that Makuria was a highly centralized state; others describe it as a confederation of thirteen loosely allied sub-kingdoms.

Although Makuria probably had already existed, at least informally, for several centuries, the first documented proof of the kingdom's existence is in an inscription from the sixth century. Originally, Makuria spanned a region along the Nile River from the Third Cataract southward to somewhere between the Fifth and Sixth Cataracts. It later expanded its territory to include land—and with it trade routes, mines, and oases—to the east and west.

It also appears that many of the Makurians' customs and practices were ancient and traditional ones. For example, the king was considered both a priest and a ruler, as was true in the Nubia of earlier centuries. In general, religious leaders very likely played other crucial roles in the government. One surviving account, for instance, describes a meeting between a Makurian king and a council of bishops to discuss a diplomatic issue.

It is also apparent that the Makurians had unusually rich traditions of art and culture. One example is the massive religious structure known as the Cathedral of Faras. When modern archaeologists discovered it, this building was completely filled with sand, which had preserved a number of paintings in remarkably good condition. Not surprisingly, these sophisticated paintings are depictions of royalty, religious leaders, and other important figures.

Other forms of art and craft both reflected traditional styles and developed their own characteristics during this time. For example, Makurian pottery of the time displayed a distinctive style, typified by the innovative use of painted animals and flowers. Some scholars maintain that the high point of Makurian pottery-making, in the mid-600s, constituted perhaps the richest pottery tradition in all of African history.

THE OTHER KINGDOMS

South of Makuria was the relatively small kingdom of Alodia. The first known reference to this land may be a rock inscription dating from the fourth century. However, it is not clear that the carving indeed refers to Alodia.

One of the few available pieces of information about this nation is that the people of Alodia rebelled frequently (although apparently not successfully) against Axum when that nation still controlled Nubian territory. Surviving documents from Axum record the punishments that were meted out, including such details as the numbers of soldiers killed and prisoners seized.

There is a similar lack of verified information about Nobatia, the northernmost kingdom. It appears, however, that it retained the ways of Egypt more than the others did. This is logical, considering that it was geographically the closest of the three to Egypt. Based on the similarity in names, there is speculation that Noubadians founded the kingdom. However, this has not been proven, and the variations in pronunciation of Nubian proper names makes clear identification difficult.

Of these three kingdoms, Makuria was the dominant force. Somewhere between the mid-600s and early 700s, it absorbed the other kingdoms, although it is likely that they remained semiautonomous. The details

Although not much is known about the kingdom of Makuria, it appears that much of their society was traditional and similar to previous ancient civilizations. The Cathedral of Faras was uncovered and revealed perfectly preserved religious paintings, including this one of a crowned archangel.

of this development are not clear. Some Arab chronicles of mid-600s mention a single state based at Dongola. Others indicate that Makuria and Nobatia remained separate and hostile for a longer time. Meanwhile, there is strong evidence—in the form of several inscriptions and writings—that Makuria had absorbed Nobatia by the mid-700s.

The merger was an important step for Nubia. For one thing, the unity of the three realms strengthened their ability to resist invaders. Furthermore, it provided a firm base for the second cornerstone in this period of Nubian history: the spread of Christianity.

THE ORIGINS OF CHRISTIAN NUBIA

As the three Nubian kingdoms developed, evolved, and merged, a relatively new religion—Christianity—was making inroads. The Christian faith had found tremendous popularity in the Roman and Byzantine empires and was rapidly spreading into northern Europe as well as into Africa.

It is almost certain that Nubia was first exposed to Christianity in the period during which Axum dominated the realm. King Ezana had become a Christian in 325 or 328, converted by missionaries from the Byzantine Empire. It appears that Ezana invaded Nubia soon after this conversion. Later in that same century, Christianity became the official religion of Axum, although Nubia resisted longer.

After it became a Christian country, Axum entered into a military and trade alliance with the Byzantine Empire. This sprawling Christian domain was the descendant of the Eastern Roman Empire, which had split off from the western half several centuries earlier. Its capital was in Constantinople (today's Istanbul), and its culture was largely Greek in origin. At the time, the Byzantines controlled much of the Middle East and the eastern Mediterranean. This included Egypt, which it had assumed from the original Roman Empire. Egypt was, at this time, not officially Christian, but it had many citizens who belonged to that faith.

The Byzantine emperor, Justinian I, was eager to convert the Nubians to Christianity. This was both a moral concern—missionary work was a fundamental part of Christian belief—and a practical one, as a matter of security along Egypt's southern border. Justinian assumed that the Nubians would be less likely to be in conflict with him if they shared a religion.

It is likely that some Christian monks and hermits from Egypt had earlier journeyed into Nobatia. However, the first definite sign there of

Christianity was the arrival of missionaries in the mid-sixth century. The religion quickly caught on after that. Quoted in P.L. Shinnie's article "Medieval Nubia," Ibn Selim el Aswani, an Arab traveler, described Soba,

The Byzantine emperor, Justinian I (*above*), was eager to bring Christianity to Nubia and convert its citizens. Christian missionaries sent to the area helped establish the religion in the sixth century.

the capital of Alodia, as having "fine buildings, spacious houses, churches with much gold, and gardens. . . . Their religion is . . . Christianity and their bishops come from the patriarch of Alexandria . . . and their books are in Greek which they translate into their own language."

THE WORK OF CHRISTIAN MISSIONARIES

During this period, the first documented Christian missionaries to Nubia journeyed there. One of the most important figures in this process was John of Ephesus, an early Church leader and historian from Syria.

As far as is known, he helped organize the first of many Christian missions into Nubia in the middle of the sixth century. A priest named Julian led this journey, at the request of and under the protection of the Byzantine emperor and his wife, the Empress Theodora. (Although John did much to organize the Nubian mission, he was busy elsewhere and did not travel to Nubia.)

The work of converting the tribes of Nubia was difficult, danger-ous, and full of personal hardship. John of Ephesus noted, for instance, the extreme heat that his missionaries had to endure. In a paper entitled "Medieval Nubia," archaeologist P.L. Shinnie quotes him speaking of Julian: "[He] used to say that, from nine o'clock until four in the after-noon, he was obliged to take refuge in caverns, full of water, where he sat undressed and girt [dressed] only in a linen garment, such as the people of the country wear."

MORE OBSTACLES

Julian and his successors had a difficult time in other, more crucial ways. Specifically, there is evidence pointing to the armed resistance Makurians mounted to deflect the Christian missionaries and preserve their ancient Meroite ways. For instance, accounts of the time state that, when Chris-tians tried to turn some of Nubia's temples into churches, the Makurians retaliated by attacking across the border into regions of Egypt that were Christian strongholds.

Nubian hostility to the missionaries showed up in other ways as well. For example, Longinus, one of Julian's successors, recorded that at one point he needed to avoid detection. He was forced to create a disguise that included a wig over his bald head. On another occasion, in order to avoid enemies, Longinus was obliged to detour far out of his way while en route to a southern region. Quoted in Stanley Mayer Burstein's book *Ancient Africa Civilizations: Kush and Axum*, John of Ephesus wrote,

> But because of the wicked devices of [the hostile Makurian king] who dwells between us, I sent my saintly father [Longinus] to the king of the Blemmys that he might conduct him thither by routes further inland; but the [ruler of Makuria] heard also of this, and set people on the look out in all the areas of his kingdom, both in the mountains and in the plains, and as far as the sea of weeds, wishing to lay hands on my father, and put a stop to the good word of God, as my father has written here to tell me.

SILKO

The first known Christian ruler of Nobatia was named Silko, and he was also the only Nobatian ruler who has been definitively identified by name. Little is known about him beyond a sixth-century inscription found in a temple called Kalabsha, near Aswan. It shows Silko on horseback, while the writing, in somewhat ungrammatical Greek, boasts of his skills as a warrior. Reprinted on a Web site maintained by Helmut Satzinger, an Austrian Egyptologist, it reads, in part:

> I, Silko, king of the Noubades and all the Ethiopians . . . warred with the Blemmyes and God gave me the victory. . . . At the first time I defeated them, they subjugated themselves to me and I made peace with them. . . .
>
> Those who contend with me—I do not let them dwell in their country unless they give me esteem and devotion. For I am, in the lower part [of the body] a lion, and in the upper part a bear. I have laid waste [the Blemmyes'] areas because they contended with me. I do not allow them to sit in the shade, but keep [them] rather in the sun outside and they did not drink water inside their houses. But my adversaries—I drag away their women and children.

Still more obstacles to Longinus, Julian, John of Ephesus, and their colleagues came from none other than rival Christian missionaries. Julian and his colleagues were associated with a branch of Christianity, originally from Egypt, known as the Coptic Church. Rival branches of the religion held differing theological beliefs and were intent on finding converts to their own church. The groups were so hostile to each other that they often resorted to sabotage.

However, despite such obstacles the Copts were the most successful of the missionaries. Archaeological evidence indicates that by the sixth century Coptic Christianity had thoroughly made its way into Nubia and become the official religion of the now-merged realms of Nobatia, Makuria, and Alodia. Nubia thus pledged loyalty to the Coptic leader known as the patriarch of Alexandria; the king of Nubia was closely allied with this priest and occasionally intervened militarily to protect him from enemies.

The conversion to Christianity, and the interaction with the Byzantines that resulted, was a major stimulus to Nubian culture. For example, the construction of buildings increased, since changing to the practice of Christianity required a substantial number of permanent buildings for use as churches and monasteries.

In time, a Christian church stood in virtually every town and village of the region. Some of these had been converted from earlier religious buildings. The construction styles of new structures, meanwhile, were drawn largely from existing building methods used in the Byzantine world, although Nubian artists and architects added many details. Among the surviving examples of this fusion of styles are the frescoes of Nubia's striking rock churches.

COPTIC INFLUENCES ON NUBIAN CULTURE

The advent of the church, and the arrival of increasing numbers of priests and other church officials, led to increased activity in other cultural aspects of Nubia as well. One of these was an increase in education for the elite classes, in particular the use of written language. By the end of the 500s A.D., the Coptic style of writing had largely replaced the old Meroitic alphabet. Written texts typically were now a combination of Greek, Egyptian Coptic, and Old Nubian.

Different offshoots of Christianity sent missionaries to Nubia in hopes of gaining followers. The most successful branch to do so was the Copts, a sect from Egypt. Coptic Christian inscriptions were found in ancient temples in Nubia (*above*).

The use of spoken language, meanwhile, was varied. In the early centuries of Christian Nubia, when the influence of the Byzantines was strong, Greek—the primary language of the Byzantines—was the main language for the Makurian elite. Egyptian Coptic was also an important spoken language, since trade and cultural links with Christian Egypt were strong. However, most of the Nubian population continued to speak mostly Old Nubian, as they had for centuries. Eventually, this language predominated, and Greek and Coptic were typically used primarily for ceremonial, religious purposes.

The Christian influence was felt in still other ways, as old Nubian traditions gave way to customs associated with Byzantine culture. For example, Nubian kings were no longer considered divine; they were instead mortal servants of God. Furthermore, the royalty of Nubia abandoned elaborate tombs and the practice of burying treasure and servants with the dead. Exceptions were made for church leaders, however; their bodies were dressed in fine robes and placed in elaborate burial chambers.

A STABLE AND PROSPEROUS PERIOD

Nubia apparently remained generally stable and prosperous during most of the centuries of Christian dominance. Several factors aided this. Among them was the lucrative trade arrangement with southern Africa and Egypt; trading in the Nubians' own highly regarded pottery production; the development of gold mines in the Red Sea Hills to the northeast; and an extended period of weather favorable to crop production.

However, there were also signs of coming trouble. Most significantly, a new religion and the warriors who carried its message were sweeping toward Nubia. This was Islam, which had taken firm hold in the Middle East and had begun to spread wildly in the years after the its primary exponent, the Prophet Muhammad, died in 632.

As did Christians, Muslims carried as an article of faith the belief that they should convert others to their religion. When they succeeded in conquering a land, peacefully or not, Islam became that land's religion. The Muslims were excellent warriors, so Islam quickly took root well beyond the Middle East.

As might be expected, they often met resistance. However, Egypt was not able to stop the Muslim warriors who attacked it. The Byzantines by now were in possession of Egypt, and conflicts on many of that empire's fronts were already stretching its resources and treasury to the breaking point. As a result, the Byzantine armies, especially in outlying parts of the empire, grew increasingly weak. Egypt was especially vulnerable, and after Islamic forces successfully laid siege to the vast and wealthy city of Alexandria in 641, Byzantine control in Egypt quickly ended.

Alexandria was heavily fortified and well stocked with food and supplies. It was able to hold out for six months before finally falling to the Muslims, and the rest of Egypt followed. All attempts to bring Egypt back under Byzantine rule failed.

Meanwhile, Nubia—which now encompassed a large area from Aswan to Khartoum and from the Libyan Desert to the Red Sea—faced the same threat. The armies of Egypt's new Muslim rulers soon reached the borders of Christian Nubia as well, only about a century after Nubia's conversion to Christianity. However, Nubia proved to be one of the few regions attacked by Muslim forces to effectively resist them, at least for the time being.

REMAINING CHRISTIAN

The failure to conquer Nubia was one of the few defeats that Arab armies suffered in the first century of Islamic expansion. Stymied in their efforts to expand south, they eventually agreed to forge a peace treaty. The terms of the agreement included stipulations that Nubia would remain Christian and that neither side would attack the other. Another agreement was that the First Cataract of the Nile would be the border between the two realms.

The peace treaty included a mutually beneficial trade arrangement. Gold, ivory, and slaves were the primary trade items from the south; textiles, ceramics, and glass came from the north. The methods of trade differed somewhat, however; traders in Lower Nubia used coins in their business, while those in Upper Nubia conducted trade primarily through barter.

This peaceful arrangement did not last long. Frequent civil wars and rebellions prevented Egypt's Muslim rulers from controlling large portions of their land. As they had in centuries past, Nubian leaders took advantage of Egypt's relative weakness and began to make raids into it.

According to one report, a Nubian army penetrated as far as Cairo in the 700s, in order to force the release of Coptic leaders who were imprisoned there, as well as a group of Christians who were being persecuted. However, this has not been proven, and, if it did happen, the raid may have been in search of treasure as much as anything else.

NUBIA BECOMES A MAJOR POWER

After Islamic armies took control of Egypt, Nubia was effectively cut off from the rest of Christendom. However, Nubia remained strong, and the outside world was recognizing Nubia's growing strength. A turning point came in 836, when a diplomatic mission headed by the son of a Nubian king traveled to the Baghdad court of the caliph who headed the Islamic empire.

Judging by accounts of the time, this mission was an important event. It indicated that Nubia was officially considered a powerful force in Middle

Eastern politics, strong enough to maintain its independence and its commitment to Christianity.

Nubia's power continued to increase in the following years. Within about a century, its leaders were confident enough to mount a major campaign into Egypt against its Muslim rulers. This proved at least partly successful, and by the mid-900s Nubia once again controlled a portion of Upper Egypt.

Many scholars consider this period, when it held sway over a large area of the Nile Valley, to be the high point in the history of Christian Nubia. However, this peak period did not last forever.

As might be expected, Muslim Egypt reacted strongly to Nubia's aggression. Arab forces advanced southward, driving the Nubians upriver, and took back control of Upper Egypt. Meanwhile, Arab culture began to enter Nubia in peaceful ways as well, as traders made increasing numbers of trips there, often settling and intermarrying.

This happened slowly but surely over the course of several centuries. In *Papers in African Prehistory*, historian Fage comments, "The hold of Christianity and the fabric of organized government [in Nubia] were both gradually eroded until . . . the Christian monarchy based at Dongola finally went under, to be replaced by a congeries [loose collection] of petty tribal principalities."

THE DECLINE OF CHRISTIAN NUBIA

The precise point at which Christian influence reached a low point is unclear. Some evidence indicates that some significant Islamic cultural influence may have appeared in the heart of Nubia by the early tenth century, with both Muslims and Christians living together there peaceably.

The validity of this amicable coexistence is supported by evidence of Arabic traders and settlers in the south. This naturally led to the cultures of the two groups becoming increasingly intermingled, with significant parts of the population becoming fluent in the languages of the other.

Another aspect of life was affected by intermarriage: property ownership. Since ancient times, Nubian tradition held that property passed from owner to nephew. (This was also true of a man's title, if he was of noble blood.) Islamic settlers who intermarried with Nubian women, however, defied this tradition and left everything to their own sons.

As a result, a great deal of property and power soon passed into Muslim hands, and the Nubian kingdom slipped even farther away from its Christian culture. In *Nubians in Egypt*, Robert A. Fernea comments, "Intermarriage, a famous instrument of diplomacy among Arab tribes long before Islam, transformed the Nubians into Muslims without the necessity of full-scale conversion."

There is considerable evidence pointing to the overall decline in the Christian community beginning as early as the tenth century. By the mid-fourteenth century, the structure of Christian Nubia was crumbling badly. The last active Christian church in the realm disappeared sometime in the sixteenth century, although Fernea notes that "most of the ecclesiastical [church-related] organization had collapsed before this." Soon, the entire region would be firmly Islamic.

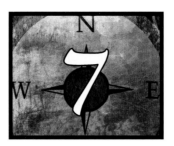

From Christian Nubia
to Islamic Nubia

As had been true for thousands of years, Nubia's fortunes in the next centuries were intimately tied to those of Egypt. The influence of Islamic Egypt, compounded by conflicts within the royal family, was slowly leading to Nubia's final collapse as a distinct culture.

It was a slow process, however. The Library of Congress book *Sudan: A Country Study* says, "[T]he arabization of the Nile Valley was a gradual process. . . . Until the thirteenth century, the Nubian kingdoms proved their resilience in maintaining political independence and their commitment to Christianity."

THE MUSLIM WORLD EXTENDS INTO EGYPT

Since the mid-seventh century, when the last peace treaty had been hammered out, the border between Egypt and Nubia, near the First Cataract, had remained more or less intact. Now, however, that treaty began to crumble, and the border they shared was seriously breached.

For example, the great Arab leader Saladin, who had defeated the Crusaders in the Holy Land, attacked northern Nubia from Egypt in the twelfth century. As the Nubian kingdom weakened, Arab leaders continued to mount military campaigns.

As might be expected, many Nubians resented the attacks, as well as the increasing numbers of Arab settlers filtering down from the north. Eventually, in 1172, the long era of peace between Egypt and Nubia ended. One dynasty of Islamic rulers, the Fatimid dynasty, died out and was

In the seventh century, pressure from the new Arab leader Saladin ended
the peace treaty between Egypt and Nubia. The new Muslim influences from
the north were following the path of Christianity and further hastened the
collapse of Nubian culture and society. Above, early Christian symbolism in a
wall mural from Nubia.

replaced by a new regime, the Ayyubid. This change in Egyptian leadership resulted in a degree of civil unrest, and Nubian soldiers were emboldened to strike back and reclaim some of their former land.

Gathering on the border between Egypt and Nubia, they first laid siege to the city of Aswan. Saladin, the first sultan (regional Muslim governor) of the Ayyubids, sent troops to defend the city. This force secured Aswan and then continued to advance, forcing the Nubians back. The Nubian armies did not give up, returning in 1173, but they were again unable to take their land back.

The Muslim army continued to penetrate farther south into Nubia and captured, among other locations, the fortress of Qasr Ibrim south of Aswan. The Egyptians converted the fortress's main church into a Muslim mosque and established a military garrison there. Qasr Ibrim then became a base for raiding the surrounding territory and holding off Nubian forces.

Evidence has been uncovered clearly showing that Nubia, under severe pressure from Egypt, was becoming increasingly unstable during this period. Vulnerable cities were often abandoned in favor of settlements high on cliffs, with defensive walls built around them. Furthermore, the people in these villages were forced to build stronger homes with hiding places where stores of grain and other precious commodities could be kept.

CHRISTIAN NUBIA DECLINES

Finally, with Nubia experiencing extreme poverty and isolation, its ruler brokered a peace treaty. This treaty lasted for less than a century. In 1272, Nubian forces again attacked, this time assaulting the town of Aidhab on the Red Sea coast. However, the Nubian state was still quite weak, with civil unrest caused by the ongoing dynastic dispute, and its assault on Egypt was unsuccessful.

The conflict continued in the following decades. In 1315, a group of Egyptian Arabs called Mamluks entered the fray. The Mamluks were former slaves and bodyguards who had ascended so high in government that they now ruled Egypt. They were able to conquer a large part of Nubia, depose the king, and install a ruler of their own—a sympathetic Nubian who had converted to Islam. In 1317, the Mamluks made an important symbolic gesture: they turned the royal Nubian palace into a mosque.

Although much of Nubia continued to resist complete Arab control, it was a losing battle. In the late fourteenth and fifteenth centuries, Nubian territory shrank to include only the region between the First and Second Cataracts. As this took place, it became increasingly difficult for the Christian faithful to resist pressure to convert to Islam.

One reason for this is that other nations refused to help defend the Nubians. Francisco Álvares, a Christian Portuguese missionary and

THE BOUNTY BROUGHT BACK BY ARAB RAIDERS

The fighting was fierce as Egyptian Muslims infiltrated Nubia and Christian influence there waned, but the rewards were great. According to an Arab writer quoted in *The Churches and Monasteries of Egypt and Some Neighbouring Countries*, edited by A.J. Butler, on one occasion a group of Arabs, probably in the 1400s, captured the city of Ibrim, laid waste to it, and brought back a fortune in war booty:

> [When] they had defeated the Nubians, they left the town in ruins; and they took the Nubians who were there prisoners. It is said that the number of Nubians was 700,000 men, women, and children; and seven hundred pigs were found there. Shams ad-Daulah [the Muslim general] commanded that the cross on the dome of the church should be burnt, and that the call to prayer by the muezzin should be chanted . . . from its summit.
>
> His troops plundered all that was there in the district and pillaged the church throughout; and they killed the pigs. And a bishop was found in the city; so he was tortured; but nothing could be found that he could give to [Shams ad-Daulah], who made him prisoner with the rest, and he was cast with them into the fortress, which is on a high hill and is exceedingly strong. Shams ad-Daulah left in the town many horsemen, and placed with them the provisions and the weapons and ammunition and tools. In the town a quantity of cotton was found, which he carried off . . . and sold for a large sum.

explorer, wrote that in the 1520s he witnessed a visit by Nubian Christians to the emperor of Ethiopia. These ambassadors pleaded with the emperor to send priests, bishops, and other members of the church to their land, in the hope that they could help preserve Christianity there. However, the emperor refused to help and suggested that the patriarch of Alexandria was the appropriate person to approach for aid.

THE EMPIRE OF THE FUNJ

There is no universally recognized end date for the Christian era in Nubia, although it can certainly be placed somewhere between the late fifteenth and early sixteenth centuries. Nonetheless, many historians regard the year 1523 as an appropriate marker. That was the year in which the Funj—at this point the ruling dynasty in northern Nubia—converted to Islam and made it the official religion of their realm. (Despite this ruling, evidence indicates that there were pockets of Christians who continued to practice their religion long afterward.)

The Funj were also sometimes called the Sennar (which was also the name of their capital city, about 180 miles [290 km] south of what is today Khartoum). They had only recently come from southern Nubia, and their ancestry owed more to central Africa than to Nubia proper. The religion of the Funj rulers had been a mix of nature worship and Christianity before they were converted to Islam.

Apparently they had at first little knowledge of classic Islamic philosophy, but they were eager to learn more and invited scholars from other regions to come and instruct them. Because of their features and their devotion to Islam, these kings were known as the Black Sultanate. They were such ardent Muslims that they sometimes even claimed to be direct descendants of the Prophet Mohammed.

In the beginning of their reign, the Funj appear in general to have been competent governors and military leaders. They were able to consolidate their power throughout Nubia and create a stable kingdom. According to the Library of Congress's book on Sudan, "The Funj stabilized the region and interposed a military bloc [zone] between the Arabs in the north, the Ethiopians in the east, and the non-Muslim blacks in the south."

The Funj empire absorbed smaller kingdoms and expanded rapidly, and its leaders were able to hold sway over much of northeast Africa for centuries. During this period Nubia prospered, in large part because much

Nubian territory continued to shrink under the constant pressure from Egypt and its Muslim influences. As Nubian control in the region dwindled, Egyptian Arabs began converting people to Islam and building religious temples like the Mosque of Sultan Hassan (*above*) in Cairo.

of it remained fertile land for farming and raising livestock. In part, this prosperity was also due to the continued exploitation of the gold mines in the Red Sea hills and the trade routes passing through the region.

THE OTTOMAN EMPIRE

The Funj empire reached the peak of its power in the mid-1600s and then began a slow decline. This waning of power was due, in part, to bickering among the royalty of the realm and its elite class. The conflict led to a period of civil unrest that made the region increasingly vulnerable.

Another reason for Nubia's vulnerability was that it no longer was the most important element in the trade route between Africa and the Mediterranean. It had been to a large degree usurped by routes that could bypass it. As a result, Nubia's economy suffered. By the early sixteenth century, the Funj were so weak that another powerful empire was able to overwhelm them.

This was the Ottoman Empire—the forerunner of what is today the nation of Turkey. The Ottomans were Islamic warriors and statesmen based in what had been the Byzantine Empire. At its peak, the Ottoman Empire sprawled across a vast realm including southeastern Europe, western Asia, and North Africa.

The Ottoman rulers coveted access to the Red Sea for military purposes, and that meant firmly establishing themselves in North Africa. Writing in *Introduction to the History of African Civilization: Precolonial Africa*, historian C. Magbaily Fyle notes that the Funj kingdom's control of northern Nubia "virtually invited the hostility of the Ottomans, who [took] control of large segments of Nubia. This brought them to the borders of the [Funj] sultanate, leading to endless friction."

Details are uncertain, but it appears that the Ottoman Empire launched its campaign against Nubia between 1538 and 1557, during the rule of Suleiman the Magnificent, considered by many to be the empire's greatest ruler. The Ottoman army attacked from Egypt, led by a Mamluk named Ozdemir Pasha. It was a hard-fought war, with both sides claiming victory in various battles. By the early seventeenth century, however, the Ottoman Empire had driven a significant way south.

The portion of Nubia that was now part of the Ottoman realm was considered equal in status to one of its Egyptian provincial districts, overseen by administrators called *kashifs*. The kashifs were, in part, responsible for collecting taxes from the Nubians, typically in the form of goods such as livestock, grain, and linen. Since this typically had to be done by force, kashifs created private armies, with slaves overseen by officials from the ranks of the ruling class.

In some ways, the Nubian kashifs were virtually independent rulers of their regions, much as the Mamluks were in Egypt. For instance, the kashifs used their private armies to enforce the observance of Islam. According to a Swiss traveler and writer, John Lewis Burckhardt, who visited the region in 1814, Nubians were typically captured as slaves if they could not prove their adherence to Islam. In his book *Travels in Nubia*, Buckhardt writes,

The Ottoman Empire launched a military campaign to occupy the lands of Nubia, further hastening the ancient kingdom's demise. Beginning with Suleiman the Magnificent, the Ottomans would control the region for centuries to come. Above, Muhammad Ali, the Ottoman ruler of Egypt and Sudan, arrives in Cairo in 1841.

I never knew any instance of a Negroe [sic] boy following the pagan worship of his father, and refusing to become Mussulman [Muslim]; though I have heard it related of many Abyssinian slaves, who, after having been converted from idolatry to the Christian religion by the Abyssinian Copts, were sold by them to the Mussulman traders.

I have been told of several of these slaves, particularly females, so steadily refusing to abjure [reject] their faith, when in the harem of a Mohammedan [Muslim], that their masters were finally obliged to sell them, in the dread of having children born of a Christian mother, which would have been a perpetual reproach [cause for criticism] to the father and his offspring.

In time the kashifs asserted their independence even more, refusing to send annual tribute to the Ottoman rulers or to guarantee safe passage through their territory above the river's First Cataract. This meant that Ottoman traders were forced to take an alternate and dangerous route through the desert.

Many Nubians, meanwhile, fled the increasing oppression of the kashifs, traveling north to Egypt or south into sub-Saharan Africa. Some settled permanently as traders or craftsmen; others became seminomadic workers on caravans.

The Ottoman Empire continued to rule Nubia until the early nineteenth century. The Ottomans' realm as a whole did not end until even later, in the early twentieth century, in the aftermath of World War I. Meanwhile, Nubia's long history during this and earlier periods helped shape the modern legacy of the region.

The Legacy of Nubia

Although a great deal has disappeared, much of the rich heritage of Nubia's ancient roots can still be seen today. One of the most important aspects of this legacy involves artifacts that have been recovered from archaeological sites.

These treasures have been closely studied, and a great deal has been learned from them. Nonetheless, new discoveries continue to provide researchers with tantalizing glimpses of Nubian history—and glimpses of how aspects of that history have carried through to the present day.

TREASURE FROM TOMBS

The most famous and arguably the most important legacy of ancient Nubia is its trove of priceless artifacts, everything from the ruins of buildings to small pieces such as tools and pottery. The excavation work needed to find these treasures is still an ongoing process. Teams of archaeologists from all over the world travel to the region to excavate and study these treasures.

As is true in Egypt, many of these artifacts—and thus much of the knowledge that scholars have been able to uncover—come from the tombs that ancient people in the region created to bury and honor their dead. The styles of these tombs varied greatly over time. Some were elaborate, filled with objects meant to help the dead make the journey to the afterlife. In some cases, specifically those of royalty and other important figures, servants and other people were sacrificed and buried along with the corpse. Others were far simpler. They were not much more elaborate than shallow graves, and the bodies were simply wrapped in cloth.

However, archaeologists are keenly aware that artifacts found in tombs provide only small pieces of the puzzle as they try to reconstruct life in ancient Nubia. Furthermore, a great deal of treasure, and therefore knowledge, is missing because the tombs have been targets for grave robbers over thousands of years.

Almost since the tombs were built, robbers have stolen their precious objects and destroyed irreplaceable wall paintings. If they had not, modern scientists would have a much fuller picture of the ancient world, and a much greater appreciation for the brilliance of its treasures. Dietrich Wildung comments, "Almost all of the royal tombs in the [Nubian cemeteries] were thoroughly plundered. Those few objects that have survived—forgotten, lost, or thrown aside by the tomb robbers—provide [only] a dull reflection of the original splendor of the tomb furnishings."

POTTERY

Among the artifacts that have survived, in tombs and elsewhere, are tools such as axes, weapons such as bows and arrows, and decorative treasures such as jewelry. Examples of pottery are perhaps the most abundant artifacts that remain from ancient times, since they were frequently buried in tombs and so have often been excellently preserved (and because they were not valuable to early robbers). Pottery is a particularly useful object of study because it served several functions. It is an art form, a craft, and a practical tool for everyday life, providing several paths of study into the daily lives of the ancient Nubians.

In the opinion of many scholars, ancient Nubian ceramics were, in general, remarkably sophisticated compared with that of other African cultures of the corresponding period. In fact, some archaeology experts argue that the manufacture of pottery in ancient Nubia was more advanced in its artistic expression, design, and function than anywhere else in the Nile Valley, including Egypt.

Hassan Hussein Idris, director of the Sudanese National Board for Antiquities and Museums, goes even further. In his opinion, Nubian pottery, at its peak periods, represents an artistic individuality as fine as anything else in all of Africa. In his preface to *Sudan: Ancient Kingdoms of the Nile*, Idris writes, "From the mid-fifth millennium B.C. to late antiquity, Sudanese pottery provides definitive masterpieces for all of African ceramics. Across three thousand years, [it] delights us with its diversity of form and unique blend of African and Egyptian aspects."

THE ASWAN HIGH DAM

Despite the work of grave robbers and other forms of destruction to ancient artifacts, not all sites—or the treasures found in them—have completely disappeared. Researchers have been successful, in many cases, in saving and studying thousands of precious objects and large-scale sites dating from the days of ancient Nubia. By far, the single largest and most important preservation project in the region's history was organized to minimize the destruction caused by Egypt's Aswan High Dam.

This dam was a huge development, built in the 1960s and 1970s, spanning the Nile River near the First Cataract. It created an immense reservoir, Lake Nasser, that permanently flooded an area of some 2,027 square miles (5,250 square km). Many of the grandest and most important archaeological ruins in Nubia would have been lost forever if nothing had been done before this massive dam and lake came into existence.

The idea of damming the Nile at Aswan was by no means new. The earliest known attempt dates from the days of Muslim occupation in the eleventh century. Much earlier, the ancient Egyptians had also undertaken projects to modify the Nile's course, creating canals that aided them in navigating the river's treacherous cataracts.

The Aswan High Dam—clearly a far more ambitious project than these earlier attempts—had a threefold objective. It would regulate the Nile's annual flooding, thus controlling the flow of water on the river. It would also create an immense reservoir, which virtually eliminated the devastating effects of drought. Furthermore, it would generate vast amounts of hydroelectric power.

THE PRICE PAID

The dam succeeded in reaching these goals and in the process transformed the entire Egyptian economy. The amount of available farmland in the Nile Valley, according to one estimate, increased fivefold. Also, the effects of drought virtually ended, since water could be held in the reservoir until it was needed. Furthermore, since the dam was completed it has produced roughly half of all the electricity used in Egypt, in the process bringing electricity for the first time to a majority of the nation's villages.

Because so few Nubian artifacts have been found, archaeologists have made efforts to minimize any damage resulting from the massive Aswan High Dam. The dam was built to harness the power of the Nile (*above*) to provide energy to the modernizing region, but it also created a huge reservoir that permanently flooded half of what was once Nubia.

However, these improvements came at a steep price. For one thing, hundreds of modern villages were flooded and an estimated 60,000–90,000 people were forced to relocate. The Aswan project also caused serious environmental problems. One of these consequences has been the loss of silt that the Nile once carried annually into the Mediterranean; the resulting lack of nutrients that sustains sea life has devastated the Egyptian fishing industry.

However, arguably the most serious impact of the Aswan High Dam was on archaeological research. When the plan was announced, archaeologists and scholars were horrified. Lake Nasser was set to flood more than half of what had once been Nubia. Dozens, perhaps hundreds, of precious, unexplored sites would be underwater forever.

An international emergency rescue operation sped into action after the project was announced. In "New Light on a Dark Kingdom," *Time* magazine writer A.T. Baker comments, "The threat inspired 30 expeditions from 25 countries to excavate frantically ahead of the advancing waters."

Thousands of experts from around the world assembled in Nubia to excavate the region's archaeological sites before the area was flooded. In her foreword to Fernea's book *Nubians in Egypt*, anthropologist Laila Shukry El Hamamsy writes, "With the help of UNESCO [the United Nations Educational, Scientific and Cultural Organization] and contributions from many nations, plans were made for the rescue of [monuments and artifacts] before the waters of the High Dam irrevocably changed the landscape."

THE GREAT TEMPLE OF ABU SIMBEL

By far the largest single undertaking by this rescue project was the preservation of a gigantic structure of immense historical value: the Great Temple of Abu Simbel. This took two years and was one of the most extensive feats of archaeological engineering in history.

Abu Simbel was the creation of the pharaoh Ramses II. It was built over the course of twenty years in the thirteenth century B.C., part of the period when Egypt firmly ruled Nubia. The ruler's intent in building Abu Simbel was to honor several important gods, as well as to commemorate himself and his favorite queen, Nefertari, and to impress and intimidate his Nubian subjects.

The temple complex is stunning. It covers some 240 acres, roughly equivalent to 11,500 football fields. On the outside front wall of the main temple, statues of the pharaoh and his queen loom some 66 feet (20 m) high.

To preserve the temple, it was first cut up into more than 2,000 large blocks. These weighed an average of 20 tons (18.14 metric tons). The pieces were then moved to a spot about 650 feet (200 m) back from its original location. This spot also lifted the temple (on an artificial mountain) so that it was roughly 200 feet (61 m) higher in elevation. The move kept Abu Simbel far enough away from what became the western bank of Lake Nasser to prevent damage.

One of the greatest treasures that archaeologists managed to save from the Aswan High Dam construction was the Great Temple of Abu Simbel. Ramses II built the temple in Nubia to honor the gods, his queen, and himself, but also to establish a presence with his Nubian subjects.

LARGE-SCALE ARTIFACTS

The Great Temple of Abu Simbel was by no means the only large-scale relic from ancient Nubia that archaeologists have preserved. Among the most important is what remains of the ancient city of Meroe, between Aswan and Khartoum. Set in a forest of acacia trees, these ruins spread out over about one square mile (2.6 square km). Still visible are what is left of a palace, surrounded by a stone wall, as well as government buildings, several small temples, and other buildings. Also still in place are heaps of waste metal, reminders that Meroe was once an important center for ironworking.

Meroe is also the location of the largest existing group of Nubian burial pyramids, about 50 in all. The dates of their construction range from about 720 to 300 B.C. Although Nubian kings adopted the practice of building pyramids from Egyptian royalty, there are clear differences in construction. For example, Nubian pyramids are typically steeper but also smaller at their bases than Egyptian pyramids. The Nubian structures rarely measure more than 26 feet (8 m) at their bases.

Among the other large-scale remnants of ancient Nubia still in existence are the ruins of about 60 churches from the Christian era. Many of these churches were destroyed or converted to mosques when Muslims first occupied the region, but a few still exist in their original forms. They were mostly built with sun-dried bricks, the most common construction material in the region, although a few, notably those at Faras and at Ghazali, are made of stone.

LINKS WITH THE PAST

Of course, many other legacies have been left from past centuries besides tangible objects. Facets of Nubia's rich history exist today in such cultural aspects as the language, customs, religion, and lifestyles of modern-day Sudan and southern Egypt. These cultural legacies directly link today's events and people with those of long, long ago.

The links of history and politics between ancient Nubia and its modern counterpart are complex. The Ottoman Empire continued to control the realm until the late 1800s. From then, under the joint rule of Egypt and the United Kingdom, it was a colony of the United Kingdom. This colonial period ended in 1956, when the region achieved independence and was officially renamed the Republic of the Sudan.

All along, Sudanese history—ancient and modern—has been extremely volatile, with more or less constant outbreaks of violence among dozens of rival tribes. The worst of the violence in recent years has been a drawn-out and ongoing civil war between the north and the oil-rich south, as well as violence between rival religious and ethnic populations in the Darfur region, in the western part of Sudan. Horrors including genocide, mutilation, rape, and the sale of women and children as slaves continue to be far too common.

THE CULTURAL LEGACIES OF ANCIENT NUBIA

This violence and tribal warfare can be seen as a kind of negative legacy. In other words, conflict is nothing new to the region (as is true elsewhere in the world, of course). But ancient Nubia has also passed down many positive cultural legacies to the present.

In some ways, for example, the 42 million people who live in Sudan today have lives that are remarkably similar, often in positive ways, to how life there must have been long ago. These lives are intimately connected with the distinctive, ancient customs, traditions, and, in many cases, languages belonging to each of the nation's roughly 400 separate tribes.

DONATED ARTIFACTS

Not all of the artifacts remaining from ancient Nubia are as large as the city of Meroe or the Great Temple of Abu Simbel. Thousands of objects, ranging from small tools and jewelry to temples, have also been uncovered and preserved. Much of this treasure is now on display in museums and institutions around the world.

Among the most important collections are in Sudan and Egypt, notably at the Nubian Museum in Aswan, the Sudan National Museum in Khartoum, and the National Museum in Cairo. Other significant collections can be seen in Harvard University's Museum of Fine Arts; the University of Pennsylvania Museum of Archaeology and Anthropology in Philadelphia; the State Collection of Egyptian Art in Munich, Germany; the Egyptian Museum in Turin, Italy; and the Egyptian Museum in Berlin, Germany.

In addition to these are some especially important artifacts that Egypt presented to several nations that had been instrumental in the Aswan preservation project. Among these treasures are four magnificent temple complexes: the Temple of Debod in Madrid, Spain; the Temple of Taffeh in Leiden, the Netherlands; the Temple of Ellessiya in Turin, Italy; and the Temple of Dendur in New York City.

The Temple of Dendur is one of the most famous and popular exhibits in New York's Metropolitan Museum of Art. It dates from about 15 B.C. To move it from Aswan to New York City, its elaborately carved walls were first disassembled into stone blocks, weighing on average about 6.5 tons (5.9 metric tons). The entire 800-ton (727 metric ton) structure was then shipped to the United States in more than 600 crates and put on display. It is housed inside the museum to protect its sandstone walls from weather damage.

One ancient legacy revolves around how people make their livings. Sudan remains overwhelmingly rural, with the vast majority of its citizens—an estimated 80 percent—making their livings raising livestock, farming, and (among some tribes) pursuing a nomadic lifestyle. Although the discovery of oil reserves has brought money in recent decades, the economy of everyday people in Sudan still relies on these ancient ways.

Another crucial component of Nubia's heritage is its religious makeup. In this regard, the last great wave of civilization that swept through the region has prevailed. Most Sudanese, an estimated 75 percent of the total population, are Muslim. (The majority of these are Sunnis, which is the official branch of Islam in Sudan.) The rest are mostly Christian or have traditional animistic (nature-worshipping) beliefs, and these people are mostly in the southern part of Sudan.

ANCIENT AND MODERN DAILY LIFE

The use of language is also an important part of the deep legacy left to Sudan by the Nubians of past centuries. Most modern-day Sudanese speak Arabic, although this is typically a unique variation on "classic" Arabic. Meanwhile, many other distinct languages are also still spoken in the region. Educated people typically speak English as well, and a great many Sudanese speak two or more languages fluently.

The most prevalent language after Arabic is called Nobiin. Like a number of other Sudanese languages, it is a form of the region's ancient language, Old Nubian. Sudan also has hundreds of local dialects. These vary from region to region and might be spoken by the residents of only one village; some Sudanese dialects are so close to each other that they are almost indistinguishable.

The legacy of ancient Nubia can be seen in many other aspects of daily life. One notable example concerns physical characteristics. The ancient Nubians who lived in this region apparently physically resembled people from further south in Africa. Evidence of this includes Egyptian portraits of them, which depict Nubians as having very dark skin and often wearing such typical African tribal decorations as golden hoop earrings and braided or extended hair. Today's Sudanese, reflecting thousands of years of intermarriage, typically have features that are a mixture of African and Arabic characteristics.

Clothing is still another example of how ancient customs remain. Although Western dress is sometimes seen today, Sudanese women typically dress in brightly colored traditional clothes, and men often wear traditional Muslim turbans and other clothing. Furthermore, some tribes still practice the ancient custom of ritual scarring to create decorative patterns.

Also reaching from the past into the present is the question of food. Sudanese food today varies considerably by location, but in general it includes ingredients and techniques from ancient Sudanese cuisine. Among the traditional ingredients still used today are goat and sheep meat, peanuts, milk and other dairy products, and rice.

These frequently combine with ingredients introduced long ago by outsiders, such as Arab traders and the various cultures that have occupied Nubia at different stages of its history. Among these "outside" foodstuffs are spices like red pepper and garlic, as well as a variety of vegetables and fruits not native to Sudan. The typical way of eating a meal is also a legacy from ancient customs. Food is typically eaten from a large, communal tray holding meats, vegetables, sauces, and condiments. Flatbread is used as a scoop for food that cannot be easily picked up.

And another cultural legacy can be seen in Sudan's buildings. In the country's rural villages, many of the old ways of building homes remain essentially unchanged since ancient times. Walls are made of unbaked mud bricks, and are sometimes decorated with bright paint. Roofs are conical and made from woven grass. Courtyards are round and open, and enclosures for animals and storage are also made in the old way. In Kerma and the Kingdom of Kush, Kendall notes, "In many respects, [views of the ruins of ancient] dwellings evoke the architecture and organization of the typical, present-day Sudanese village."

AN ONGOING SENSE OF COMMUNITY

Some of these ancient ways of Nubian culture are disappearing, especially as increasing numbers of people move to cities, like the capital Khartoum, in search of better jobs. It is estimated that nearly half of Sudan's population now lives in urban centers.

However, to a substantial degree the old tribal customs persist. They continue to play an important role in society, allowing the Sudanese to stay together and to rely on a shared culture. In *Nubians in Egypt*, anthropologist Robert A. Fernea writes,

The centuries-old influence of Nubia is still strong in modern-day Sudan, where the mud-brick village houses resemble the ruins of the structures in Kerma, the ancient capital. While Nubian culture continues to fade away, many of the old customs still exist among the people that inhabit the area.

In a world in which people are constantly being uprooted from their native communities, and where their traditional culture seems of little use in their new settings, the Nubian example is worthy of our attention. . . . the persistence of exclusively Nubian villages, repositories of a distinct culture, has helped the people at all times to retain a sense of who they are.

As a distinct culture, Nubia is long gone, either through the changes of time or the physical world. However, in a sense, it is not completely gone. Many old ways and customs still exist, and many artifacts have been uncovered from the days of antiquity. Thanks to these, modern observers can glimpse a fleeting, tantalizing look at what life must have been like in the ancient and proud civilization of Nubia.

Chronology

All dates approximate

3800– 3100 B.C.	A-Group develops
2649– 2150 B.C.	Kushite culture flourishes
1900 B.C.	Egypt domination of Nubia begins
1480 B.C.	Egypt's domination of Nubia is complete
1150 B.C.	First known references to the C-Group (Kushite culture)

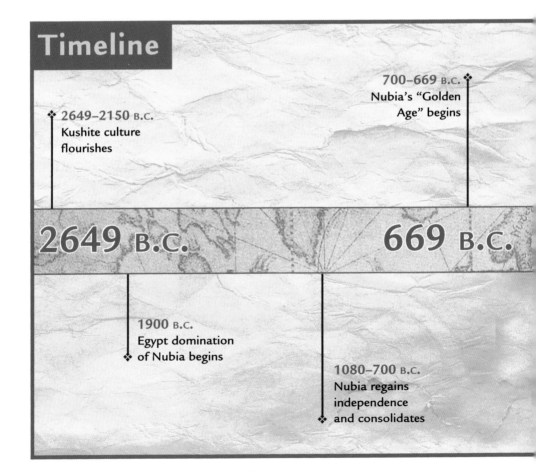

Timeline

❖ **2649–2150** B.C.
Kushite culture flourishes

700–669 B.C. ❖
Nubia's "Golden Age" begins

2649 B.C.   **669** B.C.

1900 B.C.
Egypt domination
❖ **of Nubia begins**

1080–700 B.C.
Nubia regains independence
❖ **and consolidates**

1080–700 B.C.	Egypt withdraws from Nubia; Nubia regains independence and consolidates
700–669 B.C.	Nubia invades Egypt and Nubia's "Golden Age" begins
593 B.C.	Meroitic Era begins and the Golden Age continues
300–200 B.C.	Axumites dominate Nubia
200 B.C.– 700 A.D.	Makuria is dominant kingdom in Nubia
350	Axum invades Nubia
550	Christian influence in Nubia strengthens
750 A.D.	Islamic influence strengthens
1500–1600	Islam gradually dominates Nubia
1650	Ottoman Empire dominates

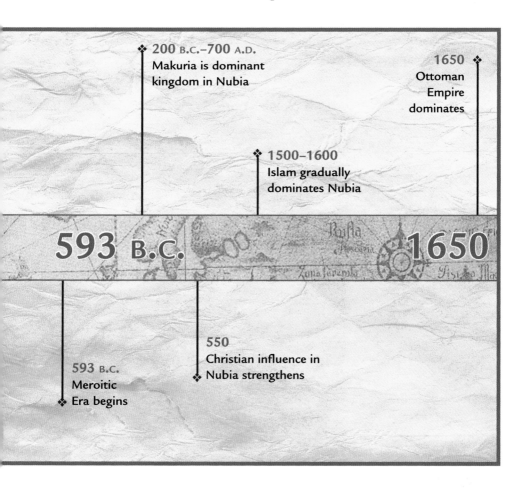

Glossary

animistic   Concerning nature worship.

archaeologist   A person who is involved in archaeology, the study of ancient civilizations.

butte   A high rock formation.

cataract   An area of shallow rapids in a river that prevent passage by boat.

dynasty   A period of rule, usually by a family.

hieroglyphic   Egyptian pictographic writing.

mercenary   Soldier for hire.

necropolis   A large-scale burial site.

nomadic   Moving from place to place (usually on a regular schedule).

oases   Areas in the desert where water can be found; plural of *oasis*.

ox   A large animal used for heavy farm work; plural *oxen*.

pharaoh   A ruler of ancient Egypt.

pygmy   Member of an African tribe noted for their small size.

scribe   Professional writer or copyist.

smelted   Describes metal that has been produced from raw ore.

stela   A rock inscription.

sub-Saharan   Africa below the northern desert region.

sultan   A regional governor in the Byzantine Empire.

tribute   A formal, often ceremonial, tax.

Bibliography

Baker, A.T. "Art: New Light on a Dark Kingdom." *Time*, Oct. 2, 1978. Available online: http://www.time.com/time/magazine/article/0,9171,948706-2,00.html.

Burstein, Stanley Mayer. *Ancient African Civilizations: Kush and Axum*. Princeton, NJ: Markus Weiner, 2000

Butler, A.J., ed. *The Churches and Monasteries of Egypt and Some Neighbouring Countries*. Oxford, England: Clarendon Press, 1895

Davidson, Basil. *Africa in History*. New York: Touchstone, 1991.

Emery, Walter B. *Lost Land Emerging*. New York: Scribner's, 1967.

Fage, J.D. *A History of Africa*. London: Routledge, 1995.

Fage, J.D., and Oliver, R.A., ed.. *Papers in African Prehistory*. Cambridge, England: Cambridge University Press, 1970.

Falola, Toyin. *Key Events in African History*. Santa Barbara: Greenwood, 2008.

Fernea, Robert A. *Nubians in Egypt*. Austin: University of Texas Press, 1973

Fyle, C. Magbaily. *Introduction to the History of African Civilization: Precolonial Africa*. Lanham, MD: University Press of America, 1999.

Greener, Leslie. *High Dam Over Nubia*. New York: Viking, 1962.

Josephy, Alvin M. *The Horizon History of Africa*. New York: American Heritage, 1971.

Kendall, Timothy. *Kerma and the Kingdom of Kush*. Washington, DC: Smithsonian Institution, 1997.

Mayell, Hillary "Rare Nubian King Statues Uncovered in Sudan." *National Geographic News,* February 27, 2003. Available online: *http://news.national-geographic.com/news/2003/02/0227_030227_sudankings.html.*

Metz, Helen Chapin, ed. *Sudan: A Country Study*. Washington, DC: Library of Congress, 1992.

Oliver, Roland. *The African Experience*. Boulder, CO: Westview Press, 2000.

Reader, John. *Africa: A Biography of the Continent*. New York: Knopf, 1997.

Wildung, Dietrich, ed. *Sudan: Ancient Kingdoms of the Nile*. Paris: Flammarion, 1997.

Web Sites

Medieval Nubia and Byzantium
http://rumkatkilise.org/nubia.htm

Nubia Museum, Numibia.net
http://www.numibia.net/nubia/meroe.htm

Silko Inscription
http://homepage.univie.ac.at/helmut.satzinger/Wurzelverzeichnis/
Silko_Inscription.html

TourEgypt.net
http://www.touregypt.net/featurestories/merenre.htm

Further Resources

Books

DiPiazza, Francesca Davis. *Sudan in Pictures*. Minneapolis: Twenty-First Century Books, 2006.

Levy, Patricia. *Cultures of the World: Sudan*. Tarrytown, NY: Marshall Cavendish, 1997.

Mann, Kenny. *African Kingdoms of the Past: Egypt, Kush, Aksum*. Parsippany, NJ: Dillon, 1997.

Roddis, Ingrid, and Miles Roddis. *Sudan*. Philadelphia: Chelsea House, 2000.

Web Sites

Dignubia
http://www.dignubia.org

Maintained by the nonprofit Educational Development Center, this site has a wealth of information as well as activities, such as a game that lets you plan an archaeological dig.

Nubia
http://www.touregypt.net/historicalessays/nubia.htm

This site, maintained by a travel organization, has detailed information and photos on the different periods of Nubia, as well as on specific subjects such as temples.

"Nubia, the Forgotten Kingdom"
http://video.google.com/videoplay?docid=9198749354303793475#

This hour-long documentary from the History Channel is a fascinating look at its subject and the efforts being made to explore its legacy.

Picture Credits

Index

About the Author

ADAM WOOG has written many books for adults, young adults, and children. He has a special interest in history and biography. Woog lives in Seattle, Washington, with his wife. They have a daughter who is at university.